Succeeding at the Top

Succeeding at the Top

A *Self-Paced Workbook for Newly Appointed CEOs and Executives*

Bernard Liebowitz, PhD, CMC

Succeeding at the Top: A Self-Paced Workbook for Newly Appointed CEOs and Executives

First published in 2010 by
Business Expert Press, LLC
222 East 46th Street, New York, NY 10017
www.businessexpertpress.com

ISBN-13: 978-1-60649-114-0 (paperback)
ISBN-10: 1-60649-114-8 (paperback)

ISBN-13: 978-1-60649-115-7 (e-book)
ISBN-10: 1-60649-115-6 (e-book)

DOI 10.4128/9781606491157

A publication in the Business Expert Press Strategic Management collection

Collection ISSN (print) 2150-9611
Collection ISSN (electronic) 2150-9646

Cover design by Jonathan Pennell.
Interior design by Scribe, Inc.

First edition: July 2010

10 9 8 7 6 5 4 3 2 1

Printed in the United States of America.

Contents

Acknowledgments

Without the experience of working with and coaching the many executives moving into new positions, this workbook could not be written. My gratitude to them is wide and deep. This workbook has benefited from the authors noted in the bibliography. They have served me well as the foreground and backdrop to my thinking. Any misinterpretations or misreadings of these references are obviously my responsibility.

The issue of "discrepancy" applies to any author and to me in this instance as well. What I think I am saying or aiming at may be at variance with what comes across to the reader. Fortunately, my colleagues who have read the various drafts have provided me the kind of feedback needed to ensure as much as possible that what I intend to say, I in fact have said and written. I am deeply appreciative of their time, thoughtfulness, and feedback. In particular, I want to acknowledge and thank John Blattner (PhD), Henry Feldman, Cindy Huey, Darrell Katz (MBA), Karen Skerrett (PhD), Bettie Subkowski, and George Vukotich (PhD).

Introduction

This workbook is designed for CEOs, executives, and senior managers who have been assigned to a new position with sufficient authority, if not an explicit mandate, to enact change. My intent is to provide a foundation for how the executive can successfully introduce change into an organization by taking into account the various barriers erected when even the notion of change is first introduced. The workbook provides a basic introduction to the dynamics of organizations that must be understood in order to introduce change successfully.

Why lump the roles of CEOs, executives, and senior managers together? It might seem at first blush that their respective ranges of authority differ enough to warrant separate accounts. That is indeed true. However, the expectations for each role usually flit about the notion of "making things better," which really means "change them." At some point in their tenure, all senior managers will be invited to effect change in their organization. They may not have the same scope of authority and accountability to effect change as this workbook's primary audience has. However, even they can profit from this workbook since it will provide background, suggestions, and questions that will broaden their perspectives on organization dynamics.

The principles for introducing and managing change are very similar for all three categories. Thus, the intent of this workbook is to present material and information that can benefit any one of these leadership categories.

This workbook's utility is limited neither to specific industries nor to specific-size companies. It can also serve as preparation for those who have not yet experienced the challenges of management but are heading that way.

This workbook is based on my experience coaching CEOs, executives, and senior managers who have been assigned to a new position from either inside or outside the organization. Translating my point of view into a self-paced program has entailed organizing the various charts I have used or developed, questions I have asked, assignments I have made, and suggestions I have offered and converting them into a general framework that can be broadly used.

Rationale

You as a newly appointed executive are generally expected either to effect change in your new assignment or to maintain the status quo. These expectations, some contradictory and some in agreement, appear from numerous sources—a firm's board, the people who have hired you, the management team, employees, customers, suppliers, and so on. If your mandate is to initiate change, then generally you as a newly appointed executive either tend to "punch it up" immediately or, on the contrary, spend too much time thinking about what you want to do before acting. Frequently it is unclear what rate of change is expected and, in some instances, how much change is to be introduced. The discrepancy between and among the expectations others, as well as you, have about change can be quite troublesome and, in fact, can be the cause of many executive failures.

The alternative to initiating change is a trap in that there is no such thing as "maintaining the status quo" when you arrive on the scene. Staff will at least expect change (even if they resist it) since you are new; your style will introduce change simply because you will be different from your predecessor; the market will demand change because it is changing all the time, and your organization will have to accommodate. The people you will report to will expect you to at least do as well as your predecessor, but really they want a better return on investment, which amounts to change.

Executives who arrive in their new positions are either promoted from within or hired from the outside. The ones brought in from the outside may come from a different division within the company, from another firm that is either in the same industry or in an entirely different industry, or from another country. Regardless of the route, any new executive will have challenges that can swamp him or her if not properly prepared. The need, then, for a self-paced workbook for newly appointed executives is based on the fact that taking over such an assignment is beset with landmines that are so well hidden that they are only recognized after the trip wires have exploded the dynamite.

Executives who have been assigned overseas have at least one additional and major issue unique to them—namely, planning for their eventual repatriation and future career. While simultaneously dealing with the challenges of a new assignment and requirements for change, expats have to take personal ownership of and responsibility for the work that goes into ensuring they are not forgotten back home. This can easily distract expats from those requirements immediately in front of them. Though being assigned overseas can be a valuable experience, it also takes the expat off the stage that principal office people are an audience to and are most immediately concerned about. Unfortunately, specific aids for the expat regarding his or her career will not be included here since that would extend the scope of this workbook.

This self-paced program is designed to assist you, the newly appointed executive, in detecting the landmines, defusing them, and creating new roadways along which your department, division, or company can advance.

Putting It Down on Paper

The most important undertaking you have in the early stages of any new assignment is learning about the organization, its culture, its people, its problems, and its strengths, as well as learning about yourself in this new context. Even if you have been promoted from within and are expected to be very knowledgeable about the organization, your perspective will change dramatically and require you to reframe what you have learned and thought. The nature of your relationships will change. Your evaluation of staff will be seen through a different pair of lenses. Your priorities will shift.

This vast amount of information that you will be absorbing can be overwhelming, contradictory, and disconnected. It will be gathered at different times from different perspectives and vantage points. Your impressions will change and your understanding will deepen. Consequently, the most important advice that you can be given in utilizing this workbook is to write down your responses to the various questions and exercises. The questions are on a website (http://www.businessexpertpress.com/Liebowitz), so you can download them to your computer.

The reason for this suggestion is simple: Unless it is written, at some future time what you will recall of your original thoughts will bear little resemblance to what these original thoughts actually were. Your retrospective on what you think you thought, did, or decided is overshadowed by subsequent events, crises, discussions, results, and so on. Consequently, what you might have learned from the discrepancy between your original and current thinking process is lost—lost not only for benefiting you as you undertake current projects but also for informing future ones.

This emphasis on "discrepancy" is extraordinarily important and arises in many different settings and situations. Learning is a matter of going from one "state of being" to another, and the amount you have learned (or not learned) is measured by the discrepancy between the two states. For example, one of the most significant ways you grow is by receiving feedback from others about yourself. This feedback measures the discrepancy between how you think you come across to others and how others in fact see you. Another example of "discrepancy" appears in the varying perceptions among colleagues and selves about an organizational issue. Understanding and awareness of the various assumptions, presuppositions, facts that are utilized or ignored, and so on that lie behind these gaps and discrepancies aid the learning process.

Preview

The first two chapters set the stage for the remainder of the book. Chapter 1 lays out the themes underlying the book—behaviors that best occur in different early stages of your appointment and how your personal style colors your entire tenure. Chapter 2 takes on the task of how we view and integrate facts and data to make decisions—in particular, the biases and shortcuts that inevitably creep into our thinking.

Undertaking a new position really starts before you agree to accept the offer. Thus, chapter 3 elaborates on the major considerations that form the basis of the decision to accept or reject an offer. It emphasizes at least two factors: the expectations, both implicit and overt, that constitute success in the eyes of the board or hiring team and your "fit" with the organization and its culture. Chapters 4, 5, and 6 detail the many tasks and considerations that appear in stages—the early stage, the middle phase, and the settling-in period. Each has distinctive tasks that are best begun in one or another stage and serve as a foundation for the succeeding stages. Chapter 7 ends the book with a review of what has preceded it.

CHAPTER 1

Underlying Themes

There are many factors contributing to success or, for that matter, failure in a takeover assignment, and generally speaking, you can never keep them all in mind simultaneously as you navigate your way through an assignment. However, several of these factors bear extra and continued consideration—errors in judgment within these categories will surely lead to failure. These are among the most prominent:

- Certain behaviors, procedures, and considerations increase the odds for success, particularly when they occur at well-timed intervals and in different phases of your early tenure.[1]
- Your general attitude toward and feelings about change, your involvement of others, your leadership, and your ability to follow can either promote or undermine what needs to get done.
- The style of thinking and decision making you and, by extension, your firm exhibit can either contribute to your success or detract from it.

The structure underlying these several themes is that your behavior, your attitude, and your decision-making style are tightly intertwined, such that a mishap or miscue in one will affect the others in significant and frequently unintended, unexpected ways.

Behavior in Phases

The time periods that are the focus of this workbook cover perhaps 3 to 5 months altogether. This period is your "initiation" to the firm and is followed by your acceptance as "the executive." The initiation period is divided into several phases and reflects the fact that certain action steps, behaviors, and decisions are most effective when they appear in certain time frames and can be decidedly ineffective (or worse) in others.[2]

The length of the initiation will be somewhat shorter when the assignment, for example, involves a turnaround situation or crisis or when you have been promoted from within the division or department. A turnaround situation or crisis demands immediate repair, frequently without the benefit of sufficient time for analysis. Being promoted from within carries with it the assumption that you already know many of the people, issues, concerns, and so on and therefore require less time than someone from the outside would need to learn these basics. Even being a former insider, however, will not inoculate you from some of the landmines that can blow up. You can use this workbook to remind you of their locations.

More fully developed timelines occur when the situation is currently stable but perhaps facing a significant future competitive challenge. However, the luxury of being able to analyze the situation in some depth, without a pressing need cramping your back, can blind you to the need to change some features sooner than later. Again, this workbook is designed to keep you aware of where these features might lurk.

In general, and regardless of the specific circumstances that might lengthen or shorten the intervals, the time periods can be grouped as follows:

- Prior to the transition
- Upon the transition and during its early stages
- The middle phase during the transition
- The implementing and "settling-in" stage

These stages form the chapters of this workbook and structure the discussion throughout.

Keep in mind that these stages overlap considerably and are recursive. An analogy is the corkscrew with a prong that keeps circling but changes its distance from the center. Thus, many of the questions that might be asked prior to the transition cannot be answered for a variety of reasons. However, determining the answers to these same questions during the early stages of the transition, and as rapidly as possible, may be crucial to your success in the assignment. Further along in your tenure, the same questions may have to be asked again because the answers will differ from their original version (e.g., as a function of the intervening success or failure of the firm, new strategic directions, and so on).

Also note that the length of each period will vary as a function of the situation. A business under considerable stress because of a competitive environment may require a much more rapid initiation process than a firm that is doing well but looking to do better.

Your Style

The second factor that can make or break your tenure concerns your implicit assumptions, feelings, and behavior best captured by a concept termed a "teachable point of view."[3] It is your attitude, your principles and values, and your viewpoint that, when reflected in your behavior, express your position regarding what it takes to succeed in business in general and in the immediate situation in particular. When both coherent and integrated, your attitude motivates and energizes people to act, it effects change, and it serves as a platform for the future.

Being new to the position means you need to know the landscape prior to planting new trees or cutting down forests. However, expressing your teachable point of view should be seen as a process that gradually and over time reflects your basic values and style. Whether you choose to be overt about it or to hide it under a bushel really doesn't matter. Your staff will recognize it either way. Therefore, it seems prudent for you to consider what your teachable point of view is and how might it contribute to, or detract from, what you want to accomplish.

The elements of such a framework include the following:[4]

- Your values
- Your concept of how a business should function and operate
- An emotional energy that makes people want to do well
- An ongoing review of the situation
- A willingness to seek the facts wherever they take you

Your Values

Your values are reflected in how you think people should act in their relationships with others. Thus, for example, scapegoating or finding someone to blame for what is going wrong not only conveys the message that avoiding responsibility is the way to get along but also discourages initiative, creativity, and enthusiasm. Taking sides is another energy zapper. It models a right-and-wrong, black-and-white way of thinking that undermines creativity and defeats team building and authentic diversity.

To the extent, then, that you look for solutions and entertain possibilities rather than offer excuses (and scapegoating is looking for excuses—that is, for someone to blame for some failure or problem) or highlight all the possible roadblocks to a solution rather than make a decision, then you convey what your value set is with regard to the behavior necessary for an organization to prosper.

This aspect of your teachable point of view and your values will appear spontaneously. It is part and parcel of who you are. It behooves you to consider what your values are and to act accordingly and consciously. Barnett and Tichy[5] give the example of Jack Welch, the former CEO of General Electric, whose teachable point of view consisted of a strong focus on developing talent and leadership while working toward a workforce consisting of "A" players only. He was very deliberate and outspoken about this point of view, which he felt to be his main responsibility. He felt that an organization consisting mostly, if not entirely, of "A" players could then successfully carry out its strategy. Whether this was a successful strategy is not the point, but rather the issue is that he deliberately and publicly structured an employee policy and institutionalized it. Employees knew where they stood, managers and supervisors knew what was expected, and executives had no doubt whom to promote.

How a Business Should Operate

Your task in the initial stage of the transition is to ask, learn, and listen more than to share and tell. Sharing your thinking is to be titrated until both your level of understanding is adequate and the current level of trust allows staff to feel free to disagree. The tricky part, of course, is assessing when your understanding is sufficient enough and the trust level is supportive enough for you to share your model of the situation. But once that level has been reached, what do you share?

How you envision the success of your organization is essential for your staff to hear. This includes ideas of how a successful business operates, including assumptions about the outside world (customers, markets, distribution channels, competition) and what occurs inside the organization (e.g., core competencies, technology, products, processes, organization design). This vision provides a stage on which your perceptions can be tested and your ideas can be challenged. It expresses your respect for your staff. Being able to integrate their viewpoints and contributions and being able to reexamine and reframe your theory of how your organization can be successful invites crucial information that might otherwise be lost. This attitude prevents "groupthink." It stalls the tendency for employees and staff to waste time trying to find out what you want to hear from them and then uncritically giving it back to you. Each recursion of your theory of the business, as informed by your staff, becomes the blueprint for the next stage in your organization's development.

Your Emotional Energy

This facet of a "teachable point of view" suggests your willingness to engage in change as necessary and needed, to implement your ideas, and to communicate the direction you want the organization to go. Emotional energy is reflected in a proactive stance that is in contrast to the attitude of an executive who lets things happen without anticipating, planning for, or addressing the future. The energy exhibited by the executive energizes her employees. We are not describing mere emotion for the sake of showing liveliness but rather an attitude that conveys the feeling that something important and significant is happening.

Ongoing Review

The most difficult bridge to cross, as indicated earlier, is the one between how you see yourself and how others see you. Part of your "teachable point of view" is your openness to getting feedback from others and learning from it. The feedback is not only about your style and the impact you are having on others but also about how you are approaching your role. No doubt you have had different assignments in your career and, since you have been selected for a CEO or senior-level position, you have been successful in them. But precisely because of your past successes, you normally tend to rely on your previous way of being successful in new situations as most of us do. Nadler[6] cites different examples of previously successful people who, in applying what worked for them in the past, failed in their new assignment. For example, they may have been brought in to fix a specific problem, but once that was accomplished, they could not steer the company in a strategic direction. Similarly, a CEO who may have been successful as head of operations in her past assignment may see the new firm's operations as the driver for the company when in fact sales would be a better candidate. Being open to reviewing your way of approaching your new organization will enhance your chances of success and will send a message to the company that taking a look at oneself and welcoming feedback are OK.

A second "teachable moment" is a willingness and eagerness to continually review how your organization is functioning. This reflects your desire to make the changes that reduce bureaucracy, facilitate information flow, and provide new opportunities that challenge people's abilities and skills and invite them to stretch. Your willingness may be best demonstrated by doing what you say you are going to do when you say you are going to do it. What happens in many organizations is that information and suggestions for change are collected, announcements are made about what changes will be made in response to the information and suggestions, but then nothing is done. Again, in most cases the early stage of a transition is not the time to make changes. You really haven't learned what has to be known about your organization. However, the very process of asking, learning, and listening in the early stages attests to the energy and attitudes you intend to bring to the organization. When you do feel confident that you know what is going on, following through on what you say you intend to do conveys a picture of someone who is proactive and involved.

Too often staff may not be clear about the criteria of performance that you are utilizing. One way of dispelling doubt is to institute a performance management system (discussed more fully in chapter 5). Essentially this is a system in which the strategy you and your staff eventually develop is translated into goals for each department and then cascaded down throughout the organization. Such a system is best monitored using specialized software. A periodic review of strategy, goals, and achievements keeps everyone informed and updated about your criteria of success. An important benefit of a performance-management program is that periodic reviews set the stage to question previous assumptions and presuppositions—if things are not working out as predicted, perhaps the assumptions are wrong and need to be modified. Having such a program in place emphasizes your commitment to ongoing review.

Since a performance-management program depends on the organization's strategy, which will take a bit of time to develop, installing such a program most likely will occur in the second phase of your initiation. By this time, you and your staff have developed a working understanding of what the firm needs. The firm should be ready for it.

Seeking the Facts

Making decisions based on facts appears as a truism—who would be against this approach? The issue however is that fact-finding is a tricky thing. It is not simply a question of marshaling facts to support an argument or a strategic direction. It may mean facing unpopular and painful facts. It may mean admitting you are wrong and, worse, short-sighted. More generally, fact-finding is a question of stepping back and looking at how decisions in the organization get made and unmade and, in particular, how you make decisions. Effective fact-finding, then, entails your willingness to go beyond, to view a decision from as many perspectives or frames as possible, to continually review "the facts" no matter how painful or embarrassing they may be to you or to others. Given that decision making is so crucial a behavior in an organization, it deserves its own chapter, which follows.

Our discussion here has focused on what you as an executive bring to the table—your style in the form of your values, understanding of business, emotional energy, and willingness to review your assumptions about the business and search for facts. The tendency in discussing style is to assume that it is immutable. In many respects, it's true that one's style cannot be changed. However, we can change our behavior. If in fact an aspect of our style is to find someone to blame immediately when an error occurs, we can learn to turn our attention to gathering evidence before criticizing. A "mechanism" that allows for this transformation involves the image we want to convey to others, our openness to looking at it, an acceptance that it indeed affects others in certain ways, and a desire to improve positively the impact our style may have on others.

We all want others to see us in a certain way. To that end we try to control others' perceptions of us by acting in ways that we think will enhance and support the image we wish to convey. Given this self-image that we want others to see, we expect certain responses on the part of others. Unfortunately, when these expected or hoped-for behaviors and responses are not forthcoming, our tendency is to project our self-image more emphatically—that is, to do even more of the same. Of course, this results in even more unwelcomed behavior. How can this vicious cycle of behavior be interrupted and stopped?

Your first step is to be clear about how you want to be perceived—that is, what image of yourself you want others to see. The next is to list others' behaviors you expect and want to see displayed. The third step is to list those positive and wanted behaviors, as well as those negative and undesirable responses that you in fact receive. Reconciling what you want to have happen and what does happen involves both a great deal of self-analysis and feedback from others.

Self-Reflection

The following exercise can aid you in your self-analysis. You might try it out using your last assignment as a reference point and also periodically through your tenure in this new assignment.

1. In Table 1.1, choose exactly 10 adjectives (no more and no less) that describe how you would like to be seen and exactly 10 adjectives (no more and no less) that you feel do not fit your self-image. Place your self-image choices in the "Am" column and those adjectives that do not fit your self-image in the "Am Not" column.
2. In reviewing both sets of adjectives, choose a label that you feel adequately expresses the self-image you would like others to see.

Table 1.1. A Listing of Adjectives to Be Used in a Self-Assessment Process

	Am	Am not		Am	Am not
Helpful			Satisfied		
Relaxed			Understanding		
Exciting			Spirited		
Assertive			Congenial		
Patient			Obedient		
Conscientious			Cheerful		
Sophisticated			Obstinate		
Persistent			Convincing		
Earnest			Responsive		
Outstanding			Neighborly		
Sympathetic			Selfish		
Loyal			Reserved		
Self-starter			Serious		
Conventional			Persevering		
Eloquent			Calm		
Cynical			Popular		
Passive			Polite		
Gentle			Dynamic		
Brave			Good-humored		
Appealing			Escapist		
Thoughtful			Generous		
Self-assured			Unobtrusive		
Steady			Daring		
Competitive			Tolerant		
Fashionable			Nice		
Neat			Compelling		
Audacious			Resolute		
Polished			Tranquil		
Fearful			Cultured		
Esteemed			Dominant		
Worrying			Respectful		
Sentimental			Nonchalant		
Adventurous			Flexible		
Easygoing			Attractive		
Unassuming			Trusting		
Good mixer			Eager		
Agreeable			Shy		
Well-liked			Fussy		
Docile			Versatile		
Demanding			Amiable		
Charitable			Diplomatic		
Persuasive			Self-centered		
Careful			Consistent		

3. List those behaviors and responses that you want others to exhibit in their interactions with you.
4. List those behaviors and responses that you actually receive.
5. Compare the two sets of responses—those you want to occur and those you don't. What do you think there is in your style, in the image you profess, that accounts for this discrepancy? What in your behavior would you want to change?

CHAPTER 2

Decision Making and Your Style

The Supreme Court appointment of Judge Sonia Sotomayor in 2009 illustrates some of the difficulties in deciding needed facts for decision making. At one time in her career (October 2001), she made the following statement at the University of California, Berkeley: "I would hope that a wise Latina woman with the richness of her experiences would more often than not reach a better conclusion than a white male who hasn't lived that life."[1] This statement appeared in the context of her speech that focused on whether people of different backgrounds, gender, and experiences would arrive at the same legal decision. In the aftermath of her nomination, she was accused of being a racist who could not function impartially in cases that would appear before her in a court of law.

Two important aspects of her statement were not given appropriate attention in the aftermath of her nomination. One had to do with the fact that she failed to specify when, how, and in what context this statement might be pertinent. One can easily imagine situations in which her statement would be applicable, but in failing to provide a context, she practically invited controversy. Her failure to pin down the context when generalizing so broadly makes it seem racially biased (and some might argue that indeed it was). The moral to be garnered from this vignette, however, is how easy it is to overgeneralize and how prone we are to doing so. Overgeneralizing can be disastrous in business. Formats like lean manufacturing, Six Sigma, business process analysis, and others are designed to guard against overgeneralizing by insisting that specifications, measurements, and performance criteria are clearly in place. Unless a generalization has context, specifications, measurements, and performance criteria, it can lead to misunderstanding or worse.

Another instructive lesson for our purposes lies with the second omission that can be attributed to commentators and critics. They generally failed to mention that a white, Protestant, middle-class male judge may be prejudiced by his background as well. In assuming that Sotomayor was prejudiced precisely because of her background, they failed to acknowledge that all of us are beholden to our backgrounds. In other words, the concept of "blind justice" has its limits in reality. There is very little absolute impartiality when humans are involved.

Well, then how can we guard against allowing our backgrounds free rein in our decision-making process? How do we ensure that our generalizations don't lead us astray? How can we make better, if not absolutely impartial, decisions? A complete treatise on decision making cannot be offered here—that would require a whole book dedicated to that one topic alone, and many books have attempted that task. What will be offered here instead are several key observations that apply to organizational change and, more specifically, to the kinds of changes an executive moving into a new position would encounter.

It goes without saying that decision making depends on the facts of the situation, but as indicated earlier, what is new about that? A fact about facts, however, is that they just don't appear out of the ether. What have to be accounted for, at least, are four issues:

1. Where do we tend to look when seeking out facts?
2. What determines where we look?
3. What influences how we look?
4. How do we make sense of the facts once we have them in hand?

Though considerable overlap exists between and among each of these issues, each possesses distinctive features. In some instances the same phenomenon can be viewed from different perspectives with different implications attached.

Where We Tend to Look for Facts: Linear Versus System Thinking

We are taught from an early age that for every effect there is a cause (one or more), and usually they are closely linked in time and space. And, if the immediate cause is not sufficient to explain the effect, perhaps going back to the "cause of the cause" will resolve the issue. Unfortunately, this type of thinking usually underlies most change efforts—if the problem is X, let's do something about X without considering what else might be entailed. The wider context within which the change is being promoted and the assumptions justifying the causal connection are given little notice. Thus, Sotomayor's failure to specify the context led to much criticism directed at her.

Events occur in a context, and decisions to be made in that context must take this observation into account in order to produce the most benefit. A context can be seen as composed of different elements, each having an effect on one another. These different elements change as the context changes. Similarly, an organizational system has a set of elements that tend to stick around, each impacting the other. Since the focus here is on organizations, the term "system" is used and is to be understood as having the same structure as "context."

The decisions made within the confines of an organizational system range in scope from the minor and simple to the major and complex. They might include an event as simple as a change in the holiday schedule (at one end of a continuum) or a wide-ranging structural change in the organization (at the other end). Whatever the decision or behavior, it will have some impact on the other elements of the system. Any organization itself is a complex system, meaning that any change initiated in one part will affect all other parts, for good or bad, sooner or later. Change in one element cannot help but influence in some way all other elements—they are interconnected.

As an example, consider Figure 2.1 as showing some (but by no means all) of the issues confronting a distribution center of a large company that stored, managed, and dispersed repair parts as needed for their clients. These findings were uncovered through interviews conducted with the employees and direct observations by the author. Management was concerned with a considerable number of late and incorrect shipments. The firm itself had been growing quite rapidly. Though these problems were evident earlier when the company was smaller, growth had made them so glaring that they couldn't be ignored out of sight or mind any longer.

If we were to draw arrows depicting how any one element impacted any other, each entry would have multiple lines running through and

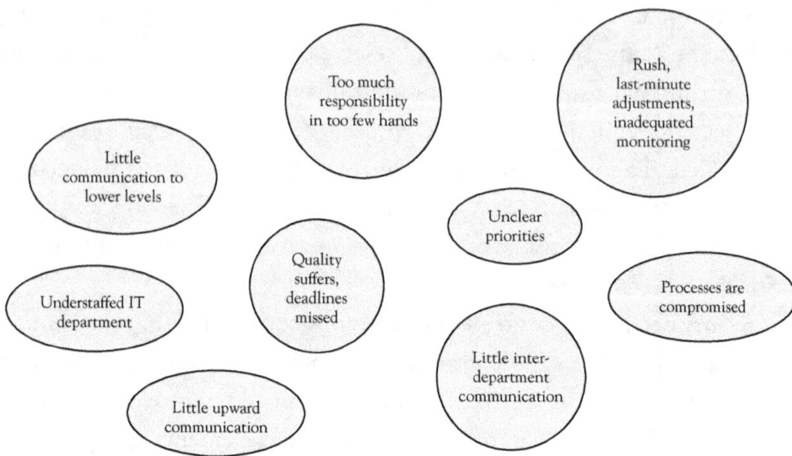

Figure 2.1. Depicting the various problems of an organization.

around it. Any attempt to introduce change into this or, for that matter, any organizational system or subsystem (e.g., a large department), must take into account these complex interactions. Failure to do so (e.g., trying to repair the most "glaring" element and ignoring the rest) leads to either failure on a grand scale or unintended consequences that cause similar headaches when they appear a bit later. Many failed change efforts can be traced back to this failure to recognize and appreciate systems.

In looking more closely at the constituents of a system, two basic dynamics appear at play: a positive self-reinforcing impetus and a negative self-correcting counterforce.[2] The terms "negative" and "positive" are to be taken as neither pejorative nor positive but rather as a positive increase in a process and a corrective (negative) influence on that process. Either can be "good" or "bad." Thus, in the previous example, as more mistakes were made in shipping and quality (a positive, self-reinforcing loop), more "work-arounds" (a negative, self-correcting loop) had to be introduced to correct the situation. Several scenarios could have developed. These two loops could have arrived at an equilibrium; that is, management would have been satisfied that the work-arounds countered the mistakes so that customers did not get too angry. Two other scenarios could also have occurred: one in which too many mistakes would have been made such that work-arounds would no longer provide a cover or one in which the work-arounds would prove too expensive for the firm.

In short, something would have to be done to deal with the problems presented. In fact, all these scenarios developed at one time or another over the years without the firm solving the basic issue once and for all.

Many loops like this one exist in all systems. They are called feedback loops because each provides information (feedback) that sets off the other. These feedback loops are linked to each other with multiple time delays (e.g., work-arounds need time to be developed, to have an effect on errors, and to be fixed themselves), nonlinearities (e.g., there is neither a direct nor an immediate connection in time between "too much responsibility in too few hands" and errors in shipping and quality), and accumulations (e.g., the number of errors has to reach a trigger point before a counterreaction in the form of a work-around is introduced).

Further, the impact an attempted change may have on the system may not be immediately apparent. In this example and at the time the author was brought in to review the situation, the errors were slowly being reduced, but this also involved the head of operations butting heads with senior management about the priorities of the firm. Some conflicting issues were the types of clients brought on board (e.g., the demands of some customers were so unrealistic that they upset shipping schedules for all customers), unrealistic shipping goals, and so on. No wonder then that the position of operations manager was seen as a temporary tenure—there were three people occupying this position within a period of 5 years, each one being let go because of "head-bumping" just as errors were being reduced. In each instance the operations manager at that time welcomed the introduced changes and wanted senior management to go further in changing other more glaring system problems, but management did not agree.

Another characteristic of systems is that there are boundary considerations that have to be taken into account. Where do you draw the boundary around a system? Too large a boundary would include elements with a minimal influence, at best, or elements that would exceed any time horizon to be effective. If you consider too tight a boundary, you eliminate important contributors to the dynamics of the system.

The company's senior management failed to look carefully at the type of customers they sought and the terms of the contracts. Thus, for example, the products of one customer were so prone to failure that the demands on operations far outweighed any return on investment. The requirements of another customer regarding when shipments were to be made were unrealistic. Management's external boundary, in effect, was the border of the company itself and excluded the outside world—that is, their customers. Given that "responsibility was in too few hands," employees' feedback was not sought, priorities were not clear, and so on. The net result was management not redrawing their boundaries, much less reviewing the other raised issues. Instead, they hired a new head of operations as soon as the former began to seriously challenge them, despite increasing, but temporary, success in shipment and quality.

So given that every element in a system affects every other element, that there are feedback loops between all these elements, that the effect of a change may not show up immediately, that there are many nonlinearities in any system, that accumulations may build up before being noticed, and that where a boundary is drawn is significant to any change effort, how does someone go about introducing change in an organization?

There are many considerations that should be taken into account when introducing change. From the viewpoint of gathering information about the organization as a system (as discussed in this chapter), change involves at least the following:

- Input over time from all levels of the company
- A statement of all the issues (variables) that could interact as a function of the introduced change
- A statement about the expected rate of change for each element
- A boundary that is broad enough to encompass those elements deemed significant

Where you start the change process depends on where you look. An underlying theme of our approach to executives moving into new positions is that looking and seeing the system is first base. Getting a grip on the organization's system and its elements depends on input from many parties and groups within and frequently from outside (customers and suppliers) as well. This format is not as daunting as a first blush might reflect. In fact, by involving employees in all aspects of change efforts, it is astonishing what can be accomplished. The facts that emerge, then, will not appear as isolated instances but rather as a coherent whole over time.

The company in the previous example decided on starting at several places at once. They first had to rethink the type of customers they wanted to work with and the terms of their written contracts. They then proceeded to review management procedures, including allocating responsibility, setting priorities, and increasing communication exchanges throughout the hierarchy. Obviously this took time to implement, but implement they did and with positive results.

What Influences Where We Look: Mental Models and Assumptions

The other facet of the Sotomayor controversy had to do with the implicit assumption that white, Anglo-Saxon judges are impartial—that is, unaffected by their background in contrast to those of Hispanic descent whose background, by definition, biases their views of justice. Critics were blinded by their failure to step back and review their assumptions about impartiality and the shadow that one's background casts on our judgment, for good or bad.

Assumptions about the world form our individual views of how the world works. They serve as the bases of how, in the face of similar evidence and facts, people differ in their understandings, beliefs, judgments, and decisions they make. An assumption is a proposition that is taken for granted. They are frequently implicit and, when unexamined, can be the source of a great deal of misunderstanding between people and within organizations. Thus, for example, in the statement, "If we fix operations, everything will be OK," the assumption is that operations is the root of all our problems. The statement "The head of operations is responsible for that" may have been implicitly accepted as true in the absence of a clear delineation of his or her role and areas of responsibilities. Indicating that there is, in fact, a head of operations can lead to false assumptions about the range of responsibility he or she can command. And, as we saw in the earlier vignette, the operations manager felt constrained as to what he could expect from management. His role and position alone were not enough to allow him to fix the problem.

Another aspect of mental models that influence decision making are the implications buried in our language usage. English is very metaphoric, as Lakoff and Johnson[3] so persuasively demonstrate. The heart of metaphor is understanding and experiencing things, thoughts, and ideas, in terms of other things, thoughts, and ideas. They demonstrate how an issue can become structured in a way that directs how we subsequently will think about it.[4] For example,

> Inflation *has attacked* the foundation of our economy.
> Inflation *has pinned* us to the wall.
> Our biggest *enemy* right now is inflation.
> The dollar has *been destroyed* by inflation.
> Inflation *has robbed* me of my savings.
> Inflation *has outwitted* the best economic minds in the country.
> Inflation has *given birth* to a money-minded generation.

Inflation is being personified as an adversary, someone to destroy. This implicit assumption behind inflation as an omnipresent enemy makes it difficult to create approaches to inflation other than the ones that would "conquer" it, and even thinking of other images of inflation is difficult, given our continual exposure to the rhetoric about "inflation as the enemy." If it were seen and discussed metaphorically as "a problem to be solved" or "a wayward child," what other ways to deal with inflation might be discovered?

As another example, consider the following view of argumentation and disagreement as war, as presented by Lakoff and Johnson:[5]

> Your claims are *indefensible.*
> He *attacked every weak point* in my argument.
> I *demolished* his argument.
> He *shot down* all my arguments.

Imagine, then, a company where differences of opinion are continually experienced as a pitched battle. What becomes of new ideas, ways of conducting business, products, and projects? Such a culture would surely discourage innovation where guarantees of success are in short supply.

Metaphoric thinking can also underlie assumptions about how specific parts of organizations work. The operations team in the previous example was seen as the "weak link" of the organization. It was referred to as the "old man of the organization," the "leak in the system," "the feebles." In other words, the metaphor defined the team as the relic of the system, implying nothing they did could work because they were too old, decrepit, and stuck in their old ways. They were seen as the weak link of the organization. Consider, then, how the operations team was related to, how people interacted with them, and how people talked about them.

A more broad and expansive use of metaphor affects assumptions about organizations in general, as described by Morgan.[6] Organizations in their entirety can be viewed metaphorically as machines, organisms, brains, cultures, power systems, psychic prisons, instruments of domination, and so on. When an organization is viewed in any one of these metaphorical constructions, consider how behavior, judgment, and decision making would be similarly influenced. To illustrate, assume management treats its organization metaphorically as a "brain," and this is the mental model entertained in their thinking and behavior with respect to the organization. A "brain" conveys the image of a computer or telephone switchboard[7] through which information passes to various locations within the company, from which people receive information and do something with it. An exclusive emphasis on this metaphor can result in minimizing the human touch. People are expected to "send and receive"—that is, to receive instructions and to do their work. Deviance from this standard is a "breakdown" in need of repair.

Contrast the "brain" metaphor with the organization as "culture."[8] A "culture," defined loosely as "how we do things around here," has norms and standards of behavior such as those embodied in "we are a family here," "we are the best in our industry," or "we work hard and have fun doing it."

The point to be made here is that all these metaphors contain important ingredients of any organization. An organization is a "brain" as well as a "culture"; it is an "organism" and a "machine." The difficulty resides in our reliance on one metaphor to fuel our mental model of an organization and, therefore, to allow it to govern how we behave and react—in other words, what assumptions we utilize to fill our mental models.

Though mental models and metaphoric usage are generally seen as populating individuals' assumptive worlds, they can easily become the standard within organizations. That is to say, "arguments as war" can become pervasive throughout the organization. Treating the organization as a "brain" can become the dominant organizational approach for how employees should behave and perform. In larger organizations where the presence of many divisions or departments mitigates against a monolithic overarching culture, these mental models and assumptions may be more specific to local groupings.

What Influences How We Look: Heuristics

We are swamped daily with facts and information. Wading through them to find those most pertinent to a specific decision or sorting through them to gather those that bolster a particular argument can become nearly impossible. Applying a rational, logical decision model (and there are many of them to choose from) to assess the vast array of facts for a particular issue can be very daunting and slow. Rather than undertaking a comprehensive analysis of the facts to arrive at a decision, we tend to rely on our intuition. Bazerman and Moore[9] characterize this as "System 1 thinking" (not to be confused with our earlier discussion of systems), which is "typically fast, automatic, effortless, implicit and emotional." In contrast, "System 2 thinking" is "slower, conscious, effortful, explicit and logical."[10]

Since our intuitive way of assessing data is not bound by a strict decision-making model, our thinking becomes subject to many biases, tendencies that we accept in order to expedite decision making in the face of a potentially extensive package of data. "Heuristics, or rules of thumb, are the cognitive tools we use to simplify decision-making."[11]

Bazerman and Moore[12] group these biases into three categories: availability, representativeness, and confirmation.

The availability heuristic refers to judging events or situations that are easily remembered because they stand out. They may have been vivid or recent and, consequently, are remembered as being more frequent. For example, an individual who may have recently missed an extremely important deadline might be seen as a loafer when, in fact, his overall performance has been meeting standards. Too often performance reviews fall under the influence of this heuristic because they occur only once a year (if that). The most recent behaviors of the individuals being reviewed are more vivid and easily recalled than their earlier behaviors and dominates the reviewer's thinking, thereby biasing the review either positively or negatively.

Stereotypes are at the root of the representativeness heuristic. Given the picture we have formed about an individual or event, we tend to look for those traits that confirm our assumptions and discredit those that don't. Part and parcel of this heuristic are several key elements. We ignore base rates such that in stereotyping an individual as a loafer, we emphasize the one time he missed deadline. We ignore sample size. Included in this heuristic is the well-known bias in which we ignore "regression to the mean"; that is, the occurrence of extreme events falls back over time to the previously established average. The presumed loafer does not necessarily loaf all the time. In contrast, the person who is consistently late with his reports does not become a "go-getter" just because the report he hands in early is extremely important for a significant sale.

We tend to want to confirm our picture and interpretation of events. This confirmation heuristic is reflected in our looking for data that supports our position and ignoring evidence that does not. Included in this heuristic is the anchoring bias. An example of this bias is the executive whose background and experience is in marketing and who subsequently views data and decisions from this point of view. This executive's background serves as an anchor in which incoming data are accepted or rejected in terms of whether they support his marketing point of view. Accompanying these biases is overconfidence in one's assessment—after all, "If I have been a successful marketing executive in the past, why wouldn't I want to use this experience in an unfamiliar situation and expect to secure the same positive outcomes," despite the fact that the new situation may not call for a marketing approach?

How We Understand What We See: Sense Making

Sense making[13] adds one more feature to the decision-making process—namely, that the actions we take, the facts we entertain and arrive at, and the point of view we develop can result in the understanding we have of the situation[14] in the first place, not that the understanding of the situation sets the stage for our subsequent actions. Sound strange?

Weick cites a dramatic illustration of this idea.[15] A study of decision making among jurors found that "jurors did not seem to first decide the harm and its extent, and then allocate blame, and then finally choose a remedy. Instead, they first decided a remedy and then decided the facts from alternative claims, then justified the remedy." In other words, "facts were made sensible retrospectively to support the jurors' choice of verdict." Actions and discussion (evaluating and weighing evidence) occurred after an individual made the decision about guilt or innocence, not before.

The battered child syndrome is currently a recognizable "disease" and no doubt has existed for a very long time. However, even though first suggested as a situation to be immediately attended to in 1946, nothing was done until 1961 when medical personnel and state laws recognized battered child syndrome. The evidence of its perniciousness had been present for a very long time. Why wasn't it given the status it demanded? One explanation offered had to do with the public's sense that anything as wicked and evil as this could not be true and therefore wasn't. The verdict was reached before the evidence was evaluated.

Similarly, resistance to change often begins with the sense "it won't work" or "it is unnecessary," and subsequent actions and developments are brought in as evidence that it didn't work and it was unnecessary. In many instances, behavior is consciously designed to ensure that "it won't work," and the results are then held up as proof that the original estimate of the change's effectiveness was accurate.

Furthermore, in choosing between distinct alternatives we tend to over-emphasize, if not "discover" after the fact, the value and benefits of the chosen option and de-emphasize those of the nonchosen alternative. Again, action (choice) precedes our appreciation of the options and justifies it.

In many ways the concept of sense making shares common elements with two of the other aspects of decision making that we have considered. It resembles mental models in that the sense-making theory has us placing data and evidence in a framework that we then accept or reject. Sense making resembles the confirmation heuristic in that it underlines how we tend to choose data and evidence that supports our initial judgments and stereotypes.

However, sense making differs in significant ways in that it goes beyond describing simply how we choose the data and facts that go into decision making. It can be understood also as a process that includes the following elements:[16]

- Identity of the decision maker
- Retrospective recall of facts, data, and events
- Creation of a sensible environment

- Social component
- An ongoing system in support of the initial sense making
- A focus on continuing extraction of supporting cues
- An emphasis on plausibility, not accuracy

Identity

One's self-concept is modified and influenced by how one imagines others see him or her. Since one's work and place of employment are a very important part of one's identify, how the one imagines others, that is, nonemployees of the company, view the organization for which he or she works becomes significant. If one's place of employment has a negative image in the community, its employees feel tarred with the same brush. Their self-image suffers ("If I stay employed in the firm, what does that say about me?"). In other situations, maintaining a positive self-image may necessitate viewing our organizations as "better." This can be seen in the attitude of "not invented here"—that is, in presuming that if a product, process, or project was created elsewhere, it should not be adopted in our organization. It is as if adopting a process first used or invented elsewhere would diminish the firm's management of a positive view of self.

Retrospective Recall

The assumption that people know what they think only after they have acted in some way implies that these past behaviors are remembered as having unfolded in such a way as to give evidence for what we believe or think. An example[17] of this was the persistence of an organization to retain labor-intensive methods of hand finishing clothes that had originated earlier because of skilled labor in the immediate area of a business. Technology had made this method obsolete and allowed competitors to pass the business in both quality, cost, and delivery time. The business, however, justified their process by thinking of it as a "high-quality" manufacturing process. The company, in preserving its original way of doing things, has simply redefined why their way is the correct way.

The same process is evident when a business attributes its success to the strategy it developed earlier, when, in fact, its strategy had not at all predicted the kind of success the firm achieved. In retrospect, management can pat itself on its collective back for having produced such a robust strategy.

Enactment of Sensible Environments

In organizational life people often create part of the environment that they then face and thereby determine their actions. The example cited by Weick[18] illustrates the point. Two police officers in a car can react to a teenager who gives them the finger in several ways: they can ignore the incident, they can stop and arrest the teenager, or they can return the gesture. Each action almost predicts what the consequences of that action will be. In an organization environment, choosing one strategy over another carries with it certain actions that, by definition, are instituted as a result of the adoption of that strategy. The commitment to a strategy can preclude necessary actions that another strategy might entail unless there exists the willingness to explore what actions other strategies might entail. To entertain this desire would reflect the attitude that our chosen strategy may not be the only and best one and that looking at other possibilities will accrue to our benefit in the long run.

Social

Sense making is a social undertaking. It occurs in a setting and, as a result, is shaped by the reaction of others. These others might be imagined or physically present in one's team or in a competitor's. In adopting a strategy, an organization—that is, its management team—may be implicitly or explicitly comparing their choice with that of their competitors, ignoring how their respective situations may vastly differ and require different approaches. In addition, individuals on the management team may be evaluating their opinions against the opinions of others on the team and might withhold stating their position because it is "not as cogent" as that of the others or it may go against the prevailing mood.

The Abilene Paradox[19] is a classic example of sense making and decision making as a social undertaking. A family sitting on their porch decided to travel over 50 miles to Abilene. The day was sweltering hot, but a cool breeze made it tolerable. Some of the family members were enjoying a game of dominoes. Suddenly one of the members suggested that they get into the car and go to Abilene for dinner. The wife of the tale's author thought it a great idea and asked her husband what he thought. Since the author thought not wanting to go was out of step with the others, he agreed. Some 100 miles and 4 hours later, they returned home hot and tired. Sitting on the porch again in front of the fan that was blowing cool air, the author offered that it was a great trip. One family member, the mother-in-law, disagreed and indicated that she went along with the idea just because she thought the rest of the family wanted to go. It soon became clear that no one had wanted to go. In fact, the father-in-law who initially made the suggestion did so only because he thought that the others were bored and that the trip would introduce some excitement.

In agreeing to go, each family member imagined the others wanted to go, adjusted their desires accordingly, and contributed to a shared decision that no one really wanted.

Ongoing

As Weick indicates,[20] sense making never stops. We are always in the middle of things, though we may parse the flow of events as "before," "during," and "after." Thus we are always doing something whether we are conscious of it or not. What has gone before and what we have done before bears an influence on what we decide to do now. To what extent then might the adoption of a project be influenced by the success or failure of prior projects? For example, that a project undertaken by a department had proven unsuccessful can curse other unrelated projects that the department in question might undertake. After all, "maybe we just don't have the necessary talent or perspective." In other terms, we can't help but evaluate our current thinking in terms of our past thinking and doing.

Focus On and By Extracted Cues

We look for cues and clues that are familiar and support our interpretations and sense making. We have faith in these cues as further evidence for our understanding. Given the uncertainty inherent in the business environment in general, all the more do we look for cues that reinforce our decision and understanding, even if we have to scramble to find them. And once we find them, the more we are convinced that we were right in the first place. The overlap with the confirmation heuristic discussed earlier is quite obvious.

Plausibility, Not Accuracy

In general then, the strength of our interpretations of events and processes are more grounded in their plausibility than in their accuracy. Cues and clues engender the plausibility of our decisions and interpretions. That may be sufficient support such that going for accuracy may not feel necessary.

Summary

Assembling relevant facts in support of a decision is not an easy undertaking. Simply having an array of facts in front of you is not sufficient for good decision making. The concepts of cause-and-effect, what leads to what, the influence of heuristics and our biases on the amount of weight or value we place on data, our mental models that frame how data are entertained, and how we make sense of the facts and our interpretation of the facts serve as sieves for incoming data. These sieves allow some through and ignore others, placing data into a mental framework we have constructed to deal with our experiences.

A Tool

In the face of the multiplicity of influences on our thinking processes, what then can we look to as an aide in decision making? How can we sort out the "right facts" from those that might merely confirm our prejudices and biases? To attempt a statement-by-statement analysis of anything you or a team member might present is obviously not feasible. To review a summary of a management meeting by applying first one approach (e.g., metaphoric analysis) and then another (e.g., heuristics) is equally untenable. In either case you would never get any work done.

One way of minimizing our biases and prejudices is to bring them out on the table and assess them from a more global perspective. The following suggestions address the features of decision making thus far utilizing this perspective.

Given our tendency to make up our minds prior to considering the evidence, allowing our conclusions to take center stage makes sense. Why fight it? The suggestion is to take our "conclusions" and make them into the ideal outcomes we expect our decisions to produce. What ideal state would result were we to successfully problem solve or decide? Specifying the dimensions, characteristics, and elements of the ideal state is perhaps the most important step we could take. Essentially we are taking our preconceived, biased conclusions and laying them out baldly. This is a way of allowing all implicit assumptions to see the light of day. In doing so our biases are more easily seen, thereby permitting a realistic view of its value. A clear picture of the ideal state serves as a staging area for discovering counterproductive assumptions.

To cite an extreme example, our initial conclusion, based on our intuition and made without the benefit of evidence, is that our strategy should be a merger with another company. The ideal state would include a specification of what the merged company would look like in detail (e.g., its customers, approach to marketing, size, profit picture, and so on), how a merger would enhance our situation (in utter detail), how the merger would occur, and so on. In the process of developing this picture, changes would be made and assumptions challenged. The characteristics of the merger partner might change, the benefits that would accrue to our company might vary, and the value of the merger might lessen and yield to an alternative plan. This process might lead to rejecting the strategy or adopting the strategy with modifications.

As we have seen, there are other restraints on our decision-making prowess—biases, mental models, and assumptions that limit our field of vision. Though we can't offer specific antidotes to each one of these constraints, we can reframe the ideal state in different ways to squeeze out these cognitive limitations as much as possible.

- The "as if" frame entails people assuming the ideal state is in effect and throwing expected problems at it (because they have in the past) and challenging situations that have not cropped up yet but could conceivably do so.

- The "won't work" frame assumes that the solution is a failure. The task of the team is to analyze why it failed.
- The "effect" frame assumes the solution worked, but it had many different (both welcomed and undesirable), unexpected outcomes. These outcomes have affected the company to a great extent. The task of the team is to outline these potential effects, both positive and negative.
- The "regret" frame takes two forms:
  - Assume that the solution worked. Nevertheless, there are regrets about not having known certain "back-then-when" things. What are they?
  - Assume that the solution didn't work. What would we have wanted to know back then that would have (in some way) made a difference?

The final step is to take the findings from these frames and incorporate them into the desired solution. Often, this desired solution may not even be one of the original ones submitted to these tests but rather one that has resulted from our "frame working."

CHAPTER 3

Prior to the Transition

The kinds of planning and thinking done before the transition are among some of the most significant determinants of success in your new assignment. There are at least three issues that need to be considered in this period:

1. Your personal goals.
2. The expectations of those hiring you.
3. Your fit with the organization.

Your Personal Goals

Obviously you cannot predict the future, much less how you will fare down the road. However, you no doubt entertain some implicit or explicit assumptions about your professional future compared to your immediate opportunities. The more explicit you are about your future assumptions, the better you can evaluate whether and how this current assignment will be a contributing factor in attaining what you want. In addition, as you experience working in the new assignment, you will be in a much better position to evaluate how realistic and pertinent your initial assumptions were and to revise them in the light of your new understanding.

Expectations of the People Hiring You

Feeling honored in being offered a challenging assignment can too easily blind you to some hidden potholes in the road, in particular, the expectations of those offering you the opportunity. Even if their expectations are verbalized, there will always be some tacit assumptions about how you should conduct yourself in the new position. Uncovering these tacit assumptions can be difficult if not, at times, impossible. The people providing you with the opportunity may not be fully aware of their own assumptions; they may not want to express their unrealistic but firmly held beliefs about what you "should" be able to accomplish, and they do not want to scare you off from accepting the position.

A CEO in a firm left after only a few months of employment. The comment by the human resources representative was that he didn't fit. He was very original and creative, but he needed freedom of action and decision making. In the initial interview prior to his coming aboard, the board had ostensibly agreed that he was free to make appropriate decisions that would enhance the value of the firm. However, the definition of "appropriate" was not clarified. This failure opened the door to second-guessing on the part of the board, which drove the CEO away.

A framework that can be useful in evaluating the expectations of the board or those hiring you is to consider the following four functions of the offered position.[1]

1. Span of control deals with the resources (people, assets, money, etc.) and the decision rights regarding these resources that are available to get a job done. Control over resources can range from few to many. For example, since Wal-Mart standardizes store operations (e.g., hours of operations, merchandizing, store design, and so on), the span of control that a store executive has is narrow.

2. Span of accountability refers to those measures that will be used to assess performance.

3. Span of influence deals with the range of interpersonal interaction required to achieve goals. If the range is small, then executives don't have to deal with those outside of their immediate spheres of work. A wide span indicates interaction with and dependency on people in other units, for example, of a holding company.

4. Span of support reflects whether the executive can expect a commitment to help from others when requested. Another way of extracting from the board what they are really looking for is to focus on the executive you are replacing. What can you learn about the board's expectations of you by having them paint a picture of your predecessor?

What will complicate your perspective on the board's expectation is that frequently these will change over time. For this reason alone you will want to update your perception of their expectations on a frequent basis, particularly until the middle stages of your employment.

Your Fit With the Organization

Being able to live with and meet the expectations (both implicit and explicit) of those individuals hiring you are only partial guarantees of a successful transition. The other half of the equation is a calculation of how well you, given your style, fit the organization. It seems apparent that a limited span of control over resources would drive an entrepreneurially oriented individual to distraction, and a limited span of accountability would bore an ambitious person. Though you may have a clear mandate to change many organizational features that do not fit you, there may be some restrictions that turn out to be too abrasive and not worth accepting the position in the first place. Better to be forewarned than not.

"Fit" is the synergy between your personality style and the organization's existing culture. By now in your career, you have been given and absorbed feedback about your leadership style. You know how you prefer reports to be presented, management team to interact, and information to flow—essentially, how business is to proceed. However, in joining an organization and assuming an executive role, you are faced with a culture that has a life of its own. To what extent are you willing to take on the charge of dealing with the culture as is, modifying it or changing it completely? Let's further assume you have carte blanche from the board to effect change however you see fit—would you want to?

Culture refers to the shared beliefs, values, and norms of a group,[2] which may be explicit but are more often subtly and implicitly expressed. They can be reflected, for example, in such statements as "this is the way we do things here," "here is what is really important," "that's a no-no," and so on. Culture can be manifest[3] as rites of passage, rites of enhancement (e.g., public recognition), rites of degradation (e.g., means of discipline), rites of integration, and rites of renewal (e.g., revitalizing an organization). Each of these examples reflects organizational behaviors and attitudes that tend to coalesce into discernable cultural types.

There are as many cultural typologies discussed in the literature as there are cultural theorists, each overlapping the other in many ways. For example, Deal and Kennedy[4] paint such portraits as "The Tough Macho Guy Culture," "The Work Hard, Play Hard Culture," "The Bet Your Company Culture," and "The Process Culture." Morgan's typology[5] includes organizations as machines, organisms, brains, political systems, psychic prisons, and instruments of domination.

These typologies, despite their plurality, attempt to deal with underlying organizational features. In their own ways, they each deal with issues such as leadership, respect, and care for the individual employee; future planning, innovation, and risk preference; degree of freedom of action and decision making; and so on.[6]

Much like the process of organ compatibility, an individual and his or her style might be compatible with or might be rejected by (or reject) a culture. In assessing the ability of a candidate to fill a position, the compatibility of the existing culture with the individual needs to be considered.

An offer to a candidate to run a company in his or her own way and in his or her own style is very appealing. However, not researching "fit" even in this apparently attractive and open-ended context can lead to failure. The following vignette illustrates this point:

A candidate for a CEO position was a "big-picture thinker" with fine interpersonal skills, a team-oriented person with high standards of performance. The board expected their CEO to be self-directed and self-motivated. They presented him with a clear mandate that the organization was his show to run as he saw fit. Their only consideration was the company's growth. It was up to the CEO to decide how that was to be achieved. This laissez-faire contract was very appealing to the CEO.

The newly appointed CEO lasted in the firm only a short time before being terminated. The organization he encountered had a "cowboy" culture, a legacy from the former CEO who had promoted a no-holds-barred and aggressive tone. Managers and their respective departments acted as if they were the firm's "bread and butter." Unfortunately, the newly appointed CEO was simply unable to corral the players and impose a structure that made sense. It soon became apparent that the CEO required from the board a set of directions that he could follow, whereas the organization culture needed a firm, self-directed hand at the wheel, someone who didn't need "coddling," as the firm's HR director had noted after his dismissal.

Another firm presented two candidates to be assessed for their CEO position. The firm, a product design company, had a culture best described as "creative." Everyone in the firm was expected to present ideas, be willing to hear criticism of their ideas, and be pro-active. Processes, however, were very loosely structured, cost overruns were frequent, and quality was slipping. The two candidates were on opposite poles of "loose," one being extraordinarily creative and the other very business- and bottom-line oriented.

The author's recommendation, to the surprise of the management team, was the "button-down" candidate who would bring needed structure to the company. His 8-year reign was very positive. He imposed on the firm a culture that was much more cost-conscious, formalized, and structured where it had to be and creative when it needed to be. This was accomplished over a relatively brief period of time and, surprisingly, with little resistance. Employees knew the financial problems the firm was experiencing—the cost overruns, late project completions, periodic quality problems, and so on. He was the right person for the company at the right time. However, after 8 years, he began to hold back the firm's progress. The very style that brought coherence to the firm stood in the way of the need to change strategic direction, which required tolerance of risk, creativity, new direction, and a restructuring of the firm. None of these personal qualities fit well with the CEO's conservative style of management.

The Challenges of the Position

The tasks required of a new executive can vary considerably, as are the personality traits required to undertake them. A new executive assigned to start up a new division or business for a firm has to be a "hunter," someone who can move fast, take chances, and develop a plan without adequate information. Faced with a turnaround situation, a new executive not only has to be a "hunter" but also may have to fire people who have longevity. The executive would most likely be under a series of deadlines that have to be met. A corporate realignment entails reinventing a successful business in order to remain competitive. This requires that a new executive be diplomatic, sensitive to others (e.g., entrenched staff), but decisive with a clear picture of where the firm should go. There are a variety of other types of work situations that would require different personality traits—managing a very diverse business, influencing without authority, having difficult bosses, and so on.[7]

Two candidates were being considered for the division chief operating officer (COO) position. The division was on the brink of bankruptcy; that is, it was a turnaround situation. The following is a brief excerpt of their assessments:

"Both P. and K. are quite aggressive and assertive and are quite proactive in taking charge of a work situation. They are comfortable in directing others and are both keen on getting a job done on time. They both are willing to take risks and back up their decisions with hard work."

"P. is a risk taker whose competitive spirit will motivate others and encourage them to achieve their goals. She will try to influence people to buy into her initiatives rather than simply issue orders. However, she tends to take a scripted and somewhat inflexible approach to problems. Given only a rather modest ability to understand people and their needs, she may set overly high standards for her staff and not step back despite feedback."

"K., on the other hand, is more flexible in his approach to leadership. Given his level of empathy, he will consider the needs and skill levels of others when assigning work. He is responsive to feedback and will change his direction upon due consideration. When he encounters resistance or opposition, he will display the strength needed to take the criticism or other routine setbacks and correct his views."

Unfortunately, the author recommended that K. be given the position when in fact P. might have been more appropriate. The management staff had been in the company for a considerable period of time. They had failed to develop themselves, to question previous ownership, to broach new directions, and so on. In fact, they were not sure why the previous COO was let go despite evidence pointing to a near bankruptcy. K. was hired. Despite the need for a fast turnaround, he kept staff on too long and didn't bring in new managers as early as he might have. The firm entered bankruptcy and dissolved.

P. would have immediately challenged the executives, terminated those who couldn't see the danger signs and couldn't change, and hired new staff. Whether bankruptcy could have been averted under her guidance, we'll never know. But, what the author failed to appreciate was that P. would have responded immediately to make the necessary changes a turnaround demanded. K. may have been too "sensitive" to the sensibilities of staff.

Self-Reflection

Your Personal Goals

1. Where do you want to end up by the end of your professional career?
2. How do you see the new assignment contributing to that goal?
3. What if you don't succeed in this new assignment? What would you do to repair your lack of success? In other words, how "tragic" would failure really be?

Expectations of the People Hiring You

4. What leeway do I have to change the following:
   - Strategy
   - Personnel
   - Organizational structure
   - Market orientation
   - Product or service offerings
   - Customer makeup
5. Who will be my "go-to" person or persons? ("Go-to" person in this context refers to someone who could be approached for advice, assistance, and so on. Keep in mind there may be several such persons, each with a different offering and agenda.)

6. What were their specific concerns about the prior executive's style? What about his or her style did they appreciate? What did they not appreciate?

7. What resources, decision-making scope, and so on was that executive given?

8. What were their expectations of him or her? What was promised by the previous executive, and what was the discrepancy between the two?

9. What did the former executive do well?

10. Who was not in favor of you being selected for your new assignment? What were his or her objections to you? If someone else was favored, what about that person was attractive enough to be preferred over you?

CHAPTER 4

The Transition and Early Stages

Once you begin your tenure, you will need to attend to several issues: introducing yourself to your team, deciding who is on your team and whom you can depend on for support, and sizing up the organization. Though presented as occurring in sequence, in fact they would be best considered simultaneously.

Getting to Know You

A very important step in a successful transition is how you introduce and present yourself to your staff. Going down the line and shaking hands may be a necessity in some environments (e.g., in some foreign-based companies), but that really doesn't tell people who you are and what you are about. Setting up symbolic markers (e.g., never closing your office door to illustrate your "open-door" policy, coming dressed in classic business attire to emphasize "I mean business," and so on) also doesn't really reveal your character, much less answer the myriad of questions that your staff and executives will have about you. In fact, some of these behaviors may even be counterproductive depending on local protocol, corporate environment, or the culture of the organization.

A strong statement about yourself is a willingness to go into the "lion's den" and invite your staff to come together to interview you. The limitation on size is a function of your preference, the number of people in your division or company, and the length of time devoted to the "interview." Ask them to write out questions for you (e.g., what is your background, what are your interests, do you have a family) on slips of paper that are prepared prior to the meeting. You might ask someone either from human resources or another staff member to review the questions (since there will be many redundancies) and weed out the more personal ones (e.g., your marriage) that have nothing to do with your new role. At the interview with everyone present, you answer the questions to a comfortable degree. This approach sets the stage for your future in the new assignment.

Since this workbook is primarily oriented to American executives in American companies, attempting this type of approach in other cultures should be carefully evaluated. There is no way of predicting whether it will be seen as a positive or negative initiative in foreign venues. Ask your direct reports beforehand for their opinion about this tactic.

Several additional cautions should be observed. One set of questions will have to do with your intentions regarding change. My suggestion is that you state honestly that you don't know enough yet to have a plan, much less that you have made any decisions about the steps you intend to take. If the team that hired you has outlined their expectations and their analysis of the situation, judiciously summarizing these observations might be in order, but again, stress that your planning and analyzing is just beginning.

Another group of questions will deal with your style of managing. I would recommend that you be frank about this. If you are not and the staff's behavior feels abrasive to you because it goes against your grain, your reaction at that time will be out of the blue ("Why didn't he tell us that before?").

Once the interview is over, you might invite different people into your office for one-on-one meetings to ask how it went, how people are reacting, and what they thought the important issues were. This information will be useful in assessing the culture of the organization and analyzing the situation that you will be undertaking.

Determining the Key Players

Both prior to and in the early stages, a new executive should develop a "cognitive map" of all the key players mentioned by the board, those hiring you, and your management team. A "key" person refers to anyone, either inside or outside the organization, who can affect your position for good or ill. That might include someone who can either support your programs and decisions or have them deferred, someone who can be your cheerleader or your detractor.

If possible, try to elicit the impressions about the key players mentioned by the people in the various groups. Also, be as attentive to those key players whom everyone mentions, as well as those who are remarked about by only one or two people. Both may be crucial to your success, either in a positive or negative sense. The danger in soliciting these impressions, of course, is the strong possibility that you will assume their descriptions are entirely correct and therefore become prejudiced. On the other hand, being aware of these judgments heightens your awareness that there is something about the key player to be evaluated, with respect to your future. The fact is that those who provide you with the names of key players will have opinions about them that will seep through, either directly or implicitly. The more explicit they can be, the more conscious you are of what needs to be evaluated. The various roles these people play are listed in Table 4.1.

A "cognitive map" of key players might look like Table 4.2.

Table 4.1. Roles of the Key Players

Key players	Notes
Board members	
Predecessor	
Staff members	
Colleagues	
Customers	
Vendors	
Senior executive	
Previous alliances/Opinion makers	
HR	

Table 4.2. A Cognitive Map of Key Players

	Those who hold a positive view of me	Those who are negative about me
Those who could be helpful to me in my new position		
Those who could not be helpful to me in my new position		

Each cell of names in Table 4.2 needs to be carefully scrutinized, and a strategy for dealing with each should be pursued. For example, the cell of those who "could not be helpful" and who are "negative toward you" may not be able to directly affect you but could "bad-mouth" you to those who do count.

Another type of "cognitive map" might look like Figure 4.1.

Note how influence, either positive or negative, can be exerted indirectly through others. By using different colors to represent a positive (dark gray in this example), negative (light gray), or neutral (black) view of you, you can immediately see for yourself the influence patterns that are affecting you.

There are several reasons for developing a map of key players early on. One reason already stated is to identify those individuals who could prove resistant to any initial efforts you make as you take on the responsibilities of your new position. The resistance can take many forms: openly bad-mouthing, passively resisting, bending the ears of their colleagues, reporting to the board, and so on. Winning them over or minimizing their negative influence would obviously be in your best interest. Their behavior would, then, be less of a burden on you as you introduce new programs and processes. And, of course, depending on who they are (e.g., management staff) and given the limits placed on your authority, you may well have to replace some.

A second reason is perhaps more significant and makes more of a contribution to your success in the long run. Charting key players allows

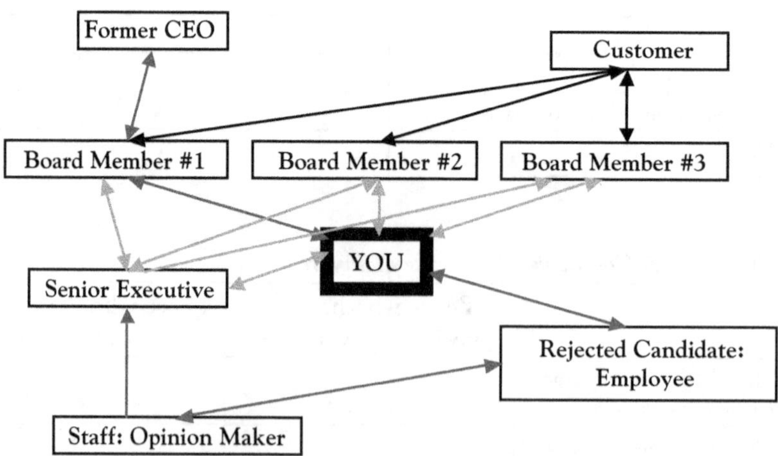

Figure 4.1. Another view of a cognitive map.

you to develop a support network, an informal group of individuals with influence at the board level who can promote your ideas and your eventual corporate strategy. Fortunately or unfortunately, performance that meets goals is no guarantee that your position as executive is secure, much less that your ideas will be objectively and impartially evaluated. Though the variety of explanations underlying dismissal despite excellent performance are endless, the one outstanding cause is the lack of a support network that can advance an executive's flag, that can speak on his or her behalf behind the lines, and that can promote that person's ideas. Keeping this network appraised of your thinking and doings, getting feedback from them, and hearing their advice will be essential to your success.

A note about the meanings of the terms "helping" and "hindering" is in order at this point since a misunderstanding can be troublesome. We all are "selfish" in one way or another; we all are looking to improve our current status (e.g., in the form of more money, prestige, feeling better about ourselves). Nothing is wrong with that, and that does not mean we are engaged in a "win–lose" game with others. Being "selfish" does not necessarily entail taking something away from someone else.

The people who can be helpful to you will be helpful to the extent that it enhances themselves in some way. One reason might be that they see you as helping the firm grow and, in doing so, supporting you makes them feel good, decreases the burden on them, and so on. It can also be a power play on their part—namely, hiring you onto management adds another member to their fan club. Someone else might feel good that they chose the best candidate, thereby justifying their excellent judgment. The reasons are many and varied. On the opposite side of the coin, not unexpectedly, those who would "hinder" you view you as a threat to their "selfishness" for whatever reason.

In either case, it behooves you to consider the "selfish" motive of each key player and honor that. For example, the individual who sees you as a boon for the company might need to hear from you on a regular basis to see how you are doing. You will need to be careful with the key person who, in choosing you, is adding players to his or her fan club—not being disloyal, but at the same time not engaging in "side taking."

Another way of saying this is that the honoring process has to be thoughtfully strategized.

Your Management Team

Shortly after you arrive on the scene, you will begin forming impressions of the people on your management team. Your evaluation will most likely focus on differentiating between those on whom you can depend to move your organization forward as opposed to those who will be laggards or worse.

You may or may not have the authority to terminate the managers reporting to you. You may even have brought along from previous assignments people whom you have worked with before. Each of these situations—retaining all, letting go of some, introducing former coworkers—or any combination thereof introduces "political" considerations. Retaining the entire management team you inherited may present opportunities for people, previously excluded from your predecessor's favored few, to vie for your "inner circle." Terminating managers can be unpopular with staff—they share a history together and change of any sort is difficult, particularly one that implicitly criticizes the past (and letting people go does just that). Bringing in your former team members can threaten the current staff.

These and many other "political" considerations are unavoidable, and their dynamics can be complex. To try to untangle the "political" dimension and the dynamics involved can be frustrating, often unrewarding, and clearly a drain on your time and energy. What to do?

Let's imagine a worst-case scenario, the intent being to suggest that any situation less onerous can benefit from exploring the most difficult. The basic assumption though that has to be made is that whoever is or becomes a member of your management team (holdovers, new personnel, your prior associates) will be treated similarly. They are all equally expected to meet goals and implement action steps.

Assume your management team is made up of an undesirable (from your point of view) person who has strong relationships upward and cannot be removed without approval from above, a popular but obstructionist individual, a former colleague whom you brought in, and so on. Let's take a look at several of these challenges.

There is no doubt that your former colleague is someone you will tend to rely on, seek advice and feedback from, and in general depend on for counsel. The issue, though, is not whether he or she becomes part of your inner circle, but rather whether you are willing to expect from everyone on your management team the same kind of performance in terms of goals and implementation. If your colleague cannot deal with his or her new cohorts and learn to work with and through them, his or her performance will suffer. Are you willing to hold your colleague accountable as you would anyone else?

The "untouchable" team members can easily become (if they have not been thus far) the ear to the ground for upper management. Your tendency could be to quite passively exclude them and their opinions from serious consideration to avoid giving them meaningful assignments—in essence, to provide them with as little grist as possible to report to their network at the top. The question here as well is, are you willing to treat the untouchable team member as you would treat others no matter how difficult this may feel?

The obnoxious-but-skilled manager will be a trial for any executive. The obstructionist can infect others, lower morale, carve the team into conflicting sects, and so on. Nevertheless, the same question about your basic stance will be raised here as well.

Let's further assume your answer, though spoken through gritted teeth, is "yes"—that you will strive to treat each equally, with respect to performance expectations and goals. Where does this take us, you might ask. What is at stake here is how you are seen in terms of objectivity, impartiality, and nonpartisanship. That you have extended even to "the least among us" (in terms of civility and likeableness) an impartial set of expectations based on performance and goal achievement will go a long way to implant in the minds of staff a positive picture of you and your intentions. The obnoxious character is usually acknowledged by a wide array of staff. How you treat this character is, surprisingly enough, an acid test of your character in the eyes of staff more than most anything else. It shows how you operate under duress.

By now in your tenure, you have begun thinking about strategy and goals. You have begun strategizing with your team. The problem then is how do you implement your strategy with the team with whom you are stuck.

This is the moment when you as an executive have to become the coach for your players—a task that is too frequently delegated to external consultants but should really be a requirement for any management position. Though covered in more detail (in chapter 6) in the context of the latter stages of your tenure, being a coach to your team really begins at the outset of your tenure.

You being or becoming a coach has several advantages that are not generally available to an external consultant. You have the opportunity to present challenges to your team members that have "real" consequences with respect to your overall strategy. And what can heat up the juices more than a challenge and a dare?

What I am suggesting is assigning meaningful but demanding tasks to each of your managers in line with your strategy, tasks that have specific goals that need to be accomplished within specific time frames and whose progress has to be periodically and publicly (in the management team setting) reported on and summarized to date during that period. Not only must you as a coach offer feedback to the individual managers about their progress in one-on-one sessions, but you must also insist that each summarize periodically and publicly on what they have learned in the process of undertaking the assignment.

Though this process is being offered to deal with the worst-case scenario, I suggest that it is applicable and desirable no matter the condition and makeup of the team.

Why the emphasis on being public?

The public reporting has several purposes. First, it helps create a sense of team in the poorly functioning management group, and it enhances the sense of team among well-functioning cohorts. In talking about one's assignment, there will be offers of assistance, suggestions, advice, and no doubt, criticism. Since everyone is operating under the same requirement to be public about the progress in their assignments, the level of undue negativism will be lowered; the manager who tends to be a naysayer might be in the "hot seat" next time. The act of sharing information has the effect of creating an "us," a team.

Second, no one wants to look bad in front of peers, thus providing the motivation to succeed. And in fact, if someone cannot live up to expectations, this becomes readily apparent. It would be difficult (but not impossible) for someone higher up to continue supporting such an individual's continued employment with the firm.

Another important value of this approach is that it lightens your burden to have to deal alone with problem managers or "politicized" situations.

The whole team is looking and is involved. As the sense of team gradually develops, negative behavior and performance are tolerated less and less.

Lastly, a considered choice of tasks that interact with each other can contribute significantly to a sense of team. This offers multiple opportunities for individual learning (in the form of feedback from peers), for accountability issues to be raised, and for collaborative effort. In those cases where overlapping and dependent responsibilities can be used as an excuse by a manager for poor performance, the learning that needs to develop is negotiating mutual expectations and goals. Even in this case the burden is back on the managers for not being able to work together for a positive outcome.

The most difficult aspect of this process is the choice of tasks. Many situations do not invite clear and specific task assignments. For example, after the chief financial officer is able to present a monthly financial statement on time and manage his department's responsibilities, what else can or should be expected of him or her? This is where your beginning appraisal of the organization comes into play and, in particular, what your management team views as financial problems. Many of the tasks that can be assigned will stem from these two sources—that is, your appraisal and your team's appraisal.

Beginning the Analysis of the Situation

A major land mine for newly assigned executives and established executives is to convey either overtly or implicitly that everything that went before was wrong and that you are here to fix it, whether it actually needs fixing. This attitude is destined to result in resistance, feet dragging, and resentment. After all, your staff helped develop the "everything that went before" for better or worse and, consequently, have some (or more) identification with it. Your wholesale rejection of their past can be seen as a rejection of them.

The alternative is to ask staff for their opinions and ideas, communicating that you want them to share the effort in making whatever changes are necessary. What makes assuming this position difficult is the need frequently felt by newly assigned executives to prove their worth, to justify their being hired, and to convey to the troops that there is a new sheriff in town. Asking for staff's opinions can appear as if you don't know what you are doing and that you are undermining your authority.

However, seeking input does not mean nor imply that you have yielded the responsibility for making decisions that are part and parcel of your mandate in your new role. If you feel that way but don't take measures to counter that sentiment in you, your role as a new executive will be severely hampered. So much of what you will accomplish is through others and with their support, all of which comes with respecting their opinions, wanting their input, and respecting their points of view. None of this necessarily needs to diminish your authority unless you allow it to.

The real test of your value to the company is your ability to analyze the situation in an actionable way while converting staff to your side of the equation. Asking staff for their perspectives will bolster that goal.

Your goal at this stage is to understand in as much detail as necessary how the company or division works with respect to the following:

- Customers (e.g., who they are, how they are enrolled, how satisfied they are with the offerings, how information about and from them is received and utilized)
- Internal processes (e.g., how products and services are "built," managed, and delivered and the role of support functions)
- Where value lies in what you are providing customers and how much that is worth to the firm
- Disconnects and problems

Interestingly enough, perhaps the most revealing source of information about the company is what staff thinks is the real reason for the previous executive leaving. He may have been terminated, he might have left because he did not feel supported, he may have left because of a more attractive offer, and so on. But these responses do not reach the level of motivation or detail that could help you in avoiding disappointment.

Taking the most apparently innocuous reason as an example—going to a more attractive position—why didn't senior management try to change his or her mind with a counteroffer? And if they had, what does your staff think weighed against the counteroffer in the mind of the executive?

The intent is to get at your staff's impressions, thoughts, and feelings whether or not they are based on facts. This information gives you additional considerations that you might not have otherwise.

However, asking these questions of staff presupposes that you have already begun building trust with your staff and they have gotten to know you to some degree. To that extent, will their responses be what they really think?

How would you go about discovering the key elements of your organization? Walking around, reading reports, and viewing sales are obvious and necessary steps. Another method not only can be very informative but also will help in building your management team. That entails discussing with your management team their responses to the questions posed in the following section. This can once again demonstrate your willingness to include them in diagnosing the situation as opposed to coming to conclusions on your.

Self-Reflection

Determining the Key Players

1. What is each person's investment in you being assigned to the new position?
2. What are their perceptions of the situation and expectations of you?
3. What kind of relationship did your predecessor enjoy (or not) with these key players?
4. Who else from within the firm or division do you think was or would liked to have been a candidate for your position?
5. Who felt responsible for the department during the handover period?
6. Who might be adversely affected by any success you may have?
7. Who will benefit from any success you may have?
8. Who is capable of influencing decisions affecting your work?

Beginning the Analysis of the Situation

9. Why was the previous executive let go ("the official reason"), and why do they "really" think he was let go? Alternatively (depending on the situation), why did the previous executive leave?
10. What did the previous executive do or fail to do?
11. What are the issues that have to be confronted?

12. What do they suggest be changed? Why?

13. Who are the key players that will be needed to effect change?

14. What has been tried before? What was successful and what unsuccessful?

15. In general, what are the strengths and weaknesses of the organization?

16. What has been the firm's strategy, including both the firm's competencies and weaknesses in carrying out the strategy?

17. What has been staff's knowledge of the strategy and its role in establishing it?

18. How supportive has staff been of the strategic intent?

19. Have people necessary to actualizing the strategy been up to the task? If not, why not?

CHAPTER 5

Developing a Convincing Scenario for Change in the Middle Phase

If you are going to introduce major changes into the system, why spend time on determining what is going on, as suggested in previous chapters? Why not just turn things around immediately?

Well, there are several ways of doing just that. You can fire everyone and start all over, but this time your way. You can threaten people to "fish with your pole or cut bait." You can point out the need for change and expect people to rush through the new door leading to paradise or its business equivalent. A turnaround situation or a firm in bankruptcy may require such harsh tactics to survive. However, in a successful business, these methods generally don't work and, if anything, they can drive an organization toward these unwelcomed states.

In contrast, what you have done thus far is set the stage for another way of introducing change:

- You established the expectations key stakeholders and superiors have of you, thereby establishing their criteria for your success.
- You determined who the key players are in the organization, those who can support your efforts as well as those who might hinder them.
- You made yourself available to staff so that they can get to know you and your style.
- You engaged staff in exploring with you the issues, problems, strengths and weaknesses, strategies, and direction of the organization as it has existed.
- You asked questions of staff that demonstrate the value you place on their opinions and indicate you seeing them as potential partners in any change effort.

The Major Tasks of the Middle Phase

Your work thus far sets the stage for the major tasks of the middle phase—namely, creating a convincing rationale for change, a rationale that captures the imagination of the workforce and that can adequately quiet, if not remove, resistance to change. What can be a first step in developing such a rationale is a small victory, a change in some aspect of the business that marshals the attention and plaudits of your team. Choosing the particular change is important in this regard. The choice not only should be part of an overall and future-directed strategy but also should present a problem in the current running of the organization. It becomes then both a motivational symbol ("This is proof that we have lived through the transition period and are once again on the road to success."), as well as the first step into the future on a course on which a great deal of time, thinking, and designing has been spent. In other words, strategy formulation comes first, followed by the selection of "the small change that convinces."

We will first explore a proposed strategy process (scenario planning, establishing goals via the Balanced Scorecard,[1] ensuring their implementation through performance management, and designing the organization to support strategy) before returning to one of your first tasks of the middle phase—selecting the "small change" that convinces your staff that the organization is ready for the future. It is important to keep in mind that the selection of the change depends on the strategic direction chosen and precedes any major innovation. All the elements of the strategy process are being presented first as a means of putting the selected change in a context. Any change, be it small or large, has ramifications that may be more easily understood with an appreciation of the strategy process under your belt. Also, this background might make a variety of choices more available to you and your team and might even make the "best" choice stand out more.

Strategy Formulation and Scenario Planning

When we talk of change, we usually think of fixing, repairing, mending, and so on, but we too infrequently pay sufficient attention to the setting, the marketplace of the future within which the organization of the future will function. We assume that the future context will be more or less like the current setting.

Resistance to organizational change draws its energy from wanting to maintain the present state. After all, if we assume the future marketplace will be the same, why change our current, successful way of doing things? But what if the "present state" is bypassed and the future becomes the magnet for thinking about the organization? Scenario planning[2] provides a platform for doing so by asking management and employees to consider different future market possibilities in which their organizations might find themselves. Staff is willing to do this because there is no threat to the status quo being imposed from the "outside." Instead, future possibilities become the occasion to consider how the firm can best meet the presented challenges.

When we talk about change management and growing our business, we too often fail to think about the kind of future business environment our firm will inhabit. We focus on our goals, new markets, capital investments, mergers, and so on, all of which makes sense to do. However, an implicit assumption we make is that the future will be the same, only better; the marketplace will be the same, only better; competition will be the same, but hopefully not any better; similar opportunities will present themselves as they have in the past. However, there are more future scenarios than "the same, only better." For example, there is "dog eat dog" in which competition has grown dramatically, challenging us in every segment of our business. A totally different future marketplace with different demands, technologies, competition, and so on is another possible future that is very likely.

We cannot predict the future, but we can imagine it. Scenario planning is a tool that allows you to peer into the future and imagine the various challenges that could confront your organization. You have assumptions, implicit or otherwise, as to what the future holds for your firm. Whatever changes you introduce now should be armed as much as possible to deal with what you and your staff can imagine will occur down the road.

There are many different ways of creating future scenarios, some of which require homework and preliminary research. A relatively simple but effective way of creating scenarios is to first consider the drivers of your industry—that is, those factors that move your marketplace, both those that are predetermined (e.g., the aging of the population) and those that are variable (e.g., interest rates). Driving forces can be put into the following categories: societal, technological, economic, political, and environmental. Cast the scenario at a time sufficiently far into the future where a clear demarcation from the present is visible, but not so far that any changes that would be made now would only be useful in the furthest reaches of your imagination. Four years or so from now is a reasonable span.

Then we can manipulate these drivers to create different future scenarios, such as "dog eat dog," "the same as now, only better," and "entirely different than now." Once you have selected the key driving forces in your industry, combine them in such a way as to produce each of the three types. Thus, for example, in designing a "dog-eat-dog" scenario, a driving force such as "the cost of steel" can be pegged at a very high rate, thus decreasing margins on your steel products. Competitors, facing the same situation in trying to sell product and secure some profit, might cut their price to gain a share of the market. In addition, we might consider interest rates as a driving force and peg them at a high level. The net result is a "dog-eating-dog" situation for a company that manufactures steel products.

For each scenario a story line is created with a history and rationale leading up to the scenario, a picture of the different strategies competitors are using in dealing with the events described, and a description of what your organization is doing to succeed in that environment. The story line and history are imagined steps that lead from now to the future event. The history can include any imagined event such as a merger, a fire that destroyed the main manufacturing plant that had to be rebuilt, new technology that changed the face of the industry, and so on. A company that houses and distributes parts used in consumer goods (e.g., electronics) for large national companies developed the following "dog-eat-dog" future based on its industry's drivers:

> Today's distribution industry is comprised of a few highly technological developed companies specializing in national distribution of diversified product lines that support the business-to-business, business-to-consumer marketplace. Utilizing technology, each of these companies exhibits a great degree of flexibility by offering their

customers a comprehensive cost-effective solution to the distribution process. Program customization is critical to success. Through a handheld device, all customers are able to access their business transactions at any point in its life. Those who differentiate themselves not only have proven to excel in traditional turnkey programs but also all capitalize on niche opportunities. Our firm has succeeded by virtually eliminating 20% of our workforce by integrating technology with manufactures, retailers, and consumers.

The question to ask after creating these scenarios is, what would our firm need to look like in each scenario in order to thrive? In general, our firm in the future will have a different appearance in each scenario. You can utilize these various pictures to answer the following: what does our firm have to do now in order to prosper, despite whatever future scenario develops? In other words, the future scenarios cover a broad array of what might occur, enough to allow us to consider current steps that we can take that would stand us in good stead no matter what develops. The answer then becomes a guide for developing a strategy and building your business.

To illustrate, a firm that manufactures broilers, fryers, and other such equipment for the chain restaurants created the following story line for a "dog-eat-dog" scenario:

In 10 years, the industry has changed to the extent that we are down to five major fast-food chains through consolidation. The food items have been reduced down to health-conscious foods and geared to the aging population. Traditional fast food as we know it is gone! Due to the economic conditions created by World War III (which the United States won), people are eating out less often due to lower discretionary incomes. The workplace in the restaurant industry has changed. The number of employees is greatly reduced due to automation of equipment and technology. The three manufacturing companies either win big or lose big!

Their next step was to consider what their organization would have to look like down the road in order to thrive in any one of the future scenarios they created. The team working on "dog eat dog" concluded that to thrive in this environment, it would need to

- develop equipment that can support more diversified menus,
- have a broader product base,
- have more intimate contact with customers (e.g., by placing representatives on site) both to determine the firm's continued viability as well as to immediately address their needs, and
- create a department devoted exclusively to exploring new technology.

The firm in this example, after each scenario was presented and discussed, noted that knowing as much as possible about the current and future needs of their clients and being immediately responsive to them was an underlying theme. In response to this finding, the firm developed cross-functional teams composed of members from each of the functional areas, each team dedicated to a different client. The intent was to have each team meet with the client regularly to discuss their needs, plans, and concerns. By having cross-functional members present at significant client meetings, not only were client questions and concerns immediately addressed by the appropriate knowledge person (e.g., an engineer replying to technical questions, a service person responding to issues regarding customer follow-up) and quality issues improved dramatically, but also a strong connection was established between the manufacturer and their clients. This connection served the manufacturer well when it came to competing with other providers.

Obviously, other kinds of scenarios can be created with different goals in mind.[3] For example, you might have four different products to bring to the market. In analyzing the receptivity of the marketplace, you might create scenarios about how each might be received. Or, in deciding whether to continue manufacturing a product, scenarios can be constructed for both the "go" and "no-go" situation to realize the impact either decision would have on the receptivity of the marketplace, the cost to the top and bottom line, and so on. Bringing this process back to the present, the question to ask is, what would we have to do now in order to be flexible enough to flourish no matter what the future holds? What can we learn from our three imagined future organizations that would help us now? This in turn can be translated into a broad overarching theme, a strategic statement that can serve as a magnet for future change and development.

Scenario planning is both most persuasive and effective when your entire staff is involved in some way—either being directly involved (usually senior managers) in the process, being asked to contribute ideas (the entire staff), or just being informed. This is not only a means of ensuring "buy-in," of promoting identification with you and your goals but also educating your staff about the realities of the marketplace.

Defining the Firm's Goals: The Balance Scorecard

The strategic statement developed from scenario planning has to be translated into goals, action steps, responsibilities, and accountabilities in order to be meaningful. The Balanced Scorecard[4] is a very creative way of sorting out goals and performance measures in keeping with an overarching strategy. This in turn can lead to those tasks that enliven strategy and bring it to the forefront of a management team's thinking.

The Balanced Scorecard takes your organization's strategic statement and invites you to consider four sets of objectives and their measures related to your strategic statement: financial, customer, internal process, and learning and growth. Figure 5.1 illustrates how a scorecard is designed.

Strategy development entails the balance of two contradictory forces[5]—a firm's focus on growth versus its efforts regarding cost effectiveness. The scorecard reflects this dichotomy in that it can be seen as divided into two, each half oriented to one or the other driver ("Productivity Strategy" or "Growth Strategy"), though there tends to be some overlap among the various variables that make up each thrust. The "Financial Perspective" deals with those goals that yield long-term shareholder value. In order to achieve these goals, a firm has to be clear about the type of customer with whom it wants to deal and for whom it can produce the most value ("Customer Perspective"). It's the "Internal Perspective" that can satisfy its customer base including operations, customer management processes (e.g., customer service), innovative capacity (e.g., developing new products and processes), and the talent that can subserve all these functions. The "Learning and Growth Perspective" refers to those intangible assets (e.g., human capital, available information, organizational culture) that, unless honored by more than lip service, can undermine the firm's best efforts.

It is important that the perspectives of the scorecard are linked to each other so that the relationships among the goals are apparent. Thus, for example, Figure 5.2 reflects the strategy of a firm whose goal is to be the most innovative and profitable in its industry.

	Productivity Strategy		Long-Term Shareholder Value		Growth Strategy
Financial Perspective	Improve Cost Structure	Increase Asset Utilization		Expand Revenue Opportunities	Enhance Customer Value
Customer Perspective			**Customer Value Proposition**		
	Price	Quality	Availability	Selection	Functionality	Service	Partnership	Brand
		Product/Service Attributes			*Relationship*	*Image*
Internal Perspective	**Operation Management Processes**	**Customer Management Processes**	**Innovation Processes**	**Regulatory and Social Processes**	
	Supply *Production* *Distribution* *Risk Management*	*Selection* *Acquisition* *Retention* *Growth*	*Opportunity ID* *R&D Portfolio* *Design/Develop* *Launch*	*Environment* *Safety & Health* *Employment* *Community*	
Learning and Growth Perspective		**Human Capital** **Information Capital** **Organization Capital**			
		Culture	Leadership	Alignment	Teamwork

Figure 5.1. A strategy map represents how the organization creates value.

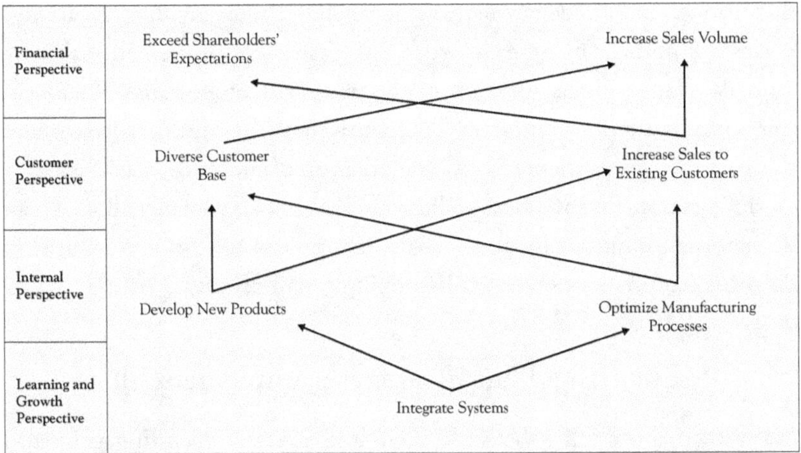

Figure 5.2. Strategy: "We will be our industry's most innovative and profitable company."

In order to do that, the management team felt its first step was to integrate its process and information technology (IT) systems, thereby optimizing its manufacturing operations. With its manufacturing processes improved, management would then be in a position to develop new products more efficiently and effectively. Given a set of new products, the firm could then attract a new and diverse customer base, as well as entice more sales from their existing customer base. The net result would be increased volume, their financial goal.

The number of goals within each category is limited only by the corporation or organization itself, not by the "logic" of goal setting. Further, each goal can have a nest of subgoals attached to it. For example, the goal of a division may be to increase sales revenues to $100 million. Nested within that goal may be subgoals of $25 million for product #1, $50 million for product #2, and another $25 million for product #3.

The only restriction on the process of goal setting is that each goal at all levels be measurable—that is, expressed numerically. This restriction often raises eyebrows, particularly around issues related to customer perception and by service-oriented firms.

For example, how can an art design department measure the creativity of its output? By sales? Well, the sales department does measure "salability," but does it measure "creativity"? The more immediate question is, how does the department define "creativity"? After some very intense and in-depth discussions, one art department came to the conclusion that "creativity" meant the number of times its work was mentioned in the national trade journals relative to the mention of the works of competitors. Obviously, this is not "creativity" but rather "competitiveness," but for this department this particular measurement was their criterion of successful creativity.

This example is intended to illustrate that in fact virtually all goals can be expressed numerically and the discussions around those that seem to defy this requirement can be enlightening for a business.

Ensuring That Strategy Is Implemented

Many companies fail to execute their strategy after spending time and money developing them. It is estimated that the vast majority of companies fall into this category. Are the companies that are reported to be in this group doing something wrong, or are they not doing something that they should be doing? In our experience it is the latter—that is, omitting a step in the process toward success. Growing firms are busy growing—they frequently don't have the time to stop and consider what is missing. When they do stop to take a breath, they discover that what is missing is performance management, a cascade of strategic goals down throughout the firm so that everyone is aware of what is expected of them. In other words, the step that is omitted is aligning each employee's goals with the firm's overall strategy. The alignment of strategic goals and the goals of each employee is the missing link that these companies fail to consider. The net result for these companies is that only a very few employees in companies truly understand their firm's strategy—that is, where the firm wants to go. No doubt this follows the observation that executive teams spend little time reviewing their strategy during the course of the year.

Note that we are talking about *performance management*, not *performance appraisal*, which is a human relations department function. Performance management is the province of the firm's CEO and C-level executives—it is directly related to the bottom line!

The bottom line of having a well-structured performance management system includes the following:

- Increased operating margins
- Quicker execution of company strategy

- A more rapid adaptation to change and the need for change
- Increased employee motivation and consequently a decrease in employee turnover
- The exposure of duplicate or redundant business initiatives
- The integration of business initiatives across departments
- Immediate correction of problems related to quality, timeliness, and inefficiencies

What gives impetus to these benefits is enhanced employee identification with the firm. If employees know what their firm's overarching strategy is and how their work contributes to the success of their organization, if they are consulted about how process improvements would support their goals, and if they are rewarded for their performance, the net result is a workforce dedicated to their company's success!

Implementing a performance management program involves the following:

- Alignment
- Cascading
- Rewarding
- Optimizing

Alignment

Once corporate goals have been established, they have to be aligned across departments. This entails ensuring that goals across the four categories are consistent, there are available resources supporting them, objectives and resources are tied to budgets, overlapping "turf" issues between departments are negotiated and resolved, and necessary and relevant information flows to all departments. Table 5.1 plots how corporate goals are distributed across a firm's departments (or divisions) and implies that each department can contribute to goals in more than one category.

Table 5.1. Departmental Contribution to Corporate Goals

	(A) Financials/profits, margins, etc.	(B) The customer	(C) Internal processes	(D) Organization learning and development corporate
Goals				
Sales				
Accounting				
Engineering				
Operations and production				

Table 5.2. The Goals of a Department

	(A) Financials/profits, margins, etc.	(B) The customer	(C) Internal processes	(D) Organization learning and development corporate
CORPORATE GOAL				
Dept'l Goal:				
How measure?				
Who measures?				
Start value?				
Aim or goal?				
Resources				
needed?				
Action steps?				
Dates?				

Table 5.3. Individual or job goals

	(A) Financials/profits, margins, etc.	(B) The customer	(C) Internal processes	(D) Organization learning and development corporate
CORPORATE GOAL				
DEPARTMENTAL GOAL				
INDIVIDUAL PERFORMANCE GOAL How measure? Who measures? Start value? Aim or goal? Resources needed? Action steps? Dates?				

Cascading of Goals

A department would utilize Table 5.2 to indicate to which goals it would contribute and to define how it would contribute to these goals.

Similar tables could be designed for each work group within each department or division, to the level of the individual. Clearly, the further downward the cascading process goes, the more tailored is the table for that specific team or individual (see Table 5.3).

These tables help employees in the various levels of the organization become aware of those activities they are expected to perform, how performance will be evaluated, and in particular, how their performance relates to corporate strategy and objectives.

Rewarding Performance

What too often occurs in many companies is that reward is only vaguely linked to performance and, even more rarely, tied to overall corporate objectives. Were they intimately linked, an employee would know those expectations and goals that have priority and the rationale for where the goals stand in the list of priorities. The employee would know from the beginning what constitutes excellent, good, and mediocre performances and could then expend his or her energies on what is truly important.

But then this kind of investment in performance should be matched by an equal investment by the company in the employee. Reward for performance would represent very tangible evidence of the firm's appreciation and consideration and can only strengthen the commitment of the employee to continued excellence for the benefit of the company. Equally important to employees is the investment the firm makes in its training and development. This is further evidence that the employee is held in esteem, that the company wants him or her to grow and develop the skills needed for advancement.

From the point of view of the supervisor or manager, a performance-management system would provide him or her the tools to clearly differentiate the levels of performance rather than relying on subjective impressions. It would allow the manager to evaluate the impact of training and development on performance and goal attainment, something that is difficult to ascertain in the absence of such a system.

Optimizing

The performanceq-management process requires an automated system that does the following:

- Is easy to use
- Is easy to learn
- Provides executives, managers, and supervisors immediate access to progress or problems
- Serves as the basis of objective feedback to employees
- Requires frequent interaction between supervisors and employees about strategies and goals and monitors the process
- Can accommodate important information about employees (e.g., 360-degree feedback, training, evaluations)
- Eliminates the need for IT involvement (they are busy enough with other issues)
- Protects the confidentiality of the individual by permitting access to authorized individuals only

With most paper-based systems, employee goals and reviews usually get filed somewhere and are infrequently reviewed, if ever. They are too often based on subjective impressions and influenced mostly by recent events rather than by objective measures. Most important, paper-based reviews do not capture "buy-in" from employees—the reviews are "pro forma" and do not convey the necessary feedback that align the employee with corporate objectives.

An automated system collates the goals and related information in a convenient online location, ready to be accessed by authorized personnel. It can quickly answer questions such as the following: Who has or has not set their goals? What teams or departments are behind in their progress? Which high-priority goals are not getting the attention they need?

In summary, the process of developing a Balanced Scorecard enables you and your team to travel and arrive at the destination at the same time. It gives everyone in the organization a common language with which to converse about business issues. It focuses them on what is important with respect to strategy. Goals, action steps, projects, and performance measures become meaningful as opposed to "something from on high" that doesn't have any particular significance to people on the line.

Organization Design

What is the best organizational design that will support your strategy? The bane of many change efforts is the lack of due consideration for how the organization is and might be structured—in particular, how and what customer information flows through the organization, how it is utilized, and who uses it. Most organizations and divisions are "siloed," where each function (e.g., manufacturing, marketing, finance, sales) has its own department within which it resides. If it were not for the fact that information between these different departments in so many organizations is either not sent, only partially sent, or sent in distorted fashion, this organization design would be fine. In fact, it has many virtues to commend it.[6]

Organizational design is structuring an organization, division, or department to optimize how it produces and supplies products and services to its customers. As a firm grows, it will (or should) redesign itself when it reaches different sales levels as well as when the nature of customer needs change. For those rapidly growing firms that have experience in redesign efforts, it can be a core competency that distinguishes them from their competitors. For those firms that are in a commodity box, it can provide a strategic advantage over competitors.

Our focus here will be on one aspect of organization design[7]—namely, the interface between the firm and its customer base. Designing an organizational-customer interface is dependent on the following:

- The kind and quality of information it gathers from its customers, suppliers, and partners
  - How the company gathers the information
  - How it interacts with each of these constituents
  - How this information flows through the organizational structures
- Who has access to information and who doesn't
- How the information is utilized in making decisions, for example, about production costs, new products, and so on
- How the information is stored for ease of use and how it is analyzed
- Whether both organizational processes and systems reflect and mirror information flow

As obvious as it seems that this list should be a priority of an executive management team's agenda, it too frequently is not. The common organizational chart usually dominates, as in Figure 5.3. Even when innovative designs are introduced (e.g., matrix structures, reduced levels of hierarchy), suggesting a sophisticated view of design considerations, the interface between the organization and its customer base is rarely entertained.

This traditional design can result in many problems:

- Conflict between departments (e.g., the perennial one between sales and operations)
- Long lead times in developing new products and services
- Quality problems, billing inaccuracies, and so on
- Inefficiencies (which are usually blamed on individuals)
- Lags in keeping up with customer demands
- Low employee morale (often related to staff not being empowered to make decisions)
- Departmental goals and performance measures not being cascaded down through the entire organization; goals stop at the top of the hierarchy without a real appreciation of how "it all fits together"

Figure 5.4 is an example of what the early stages of a business's relationship to its customers often looks like. Information about a customer is gathered by one department, which then serves as a gatekeeper for the dispersion of customer information and then parcels it out to the other departments as needed. Frequently, either the information isn't disseminated and

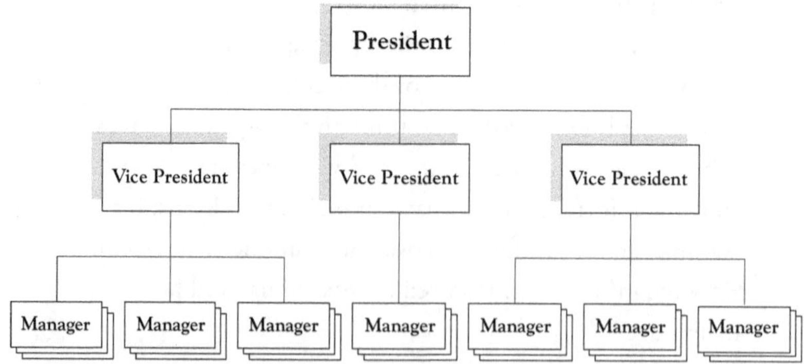

Figure 5.3. The traditional organizational chart.

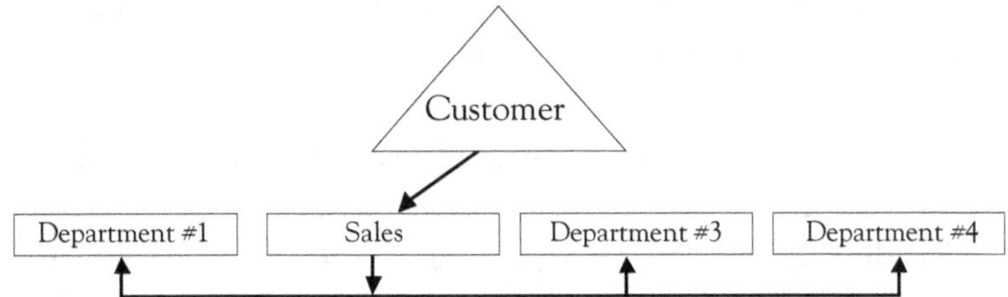

Figure 5.4. The relationship of a business in its early stages to its customer base.

discussed among the departments (it is only partially communicated) or it is presented in a way that the recipients can't readily utilize.

This structure that directs the flow of information is usually sufficient for an early stage or for a smaller company or division to function. The information needed about customers is usually limited ("Do they like it or don't they?"). However, for large and rapidly growing companies that have been accumulating competitors by the bushelful, the picture changes to multiple types of customers, with divergent and discriminating needs and interests regarding products and services. The following example demonstrates how not keeping up with customer needs can strangle an organization.

The problem: A large division of a publically traded company had been barely profitable over the last 5 years. Their sales had been stagnant during this period of time. The firm provides financial data to a broad range of companies: banks, insurance companies, corporations, and so on. The firm has been oriented to providing a range of products to their client base, products that have been seen as the standard for their industry. The chairman of the company indicated that, unless the firm grew in both sales and profit, it would be either sold or disbanded.

The scenario planning that was conducted as part of strategy formulation indicated that the customer base the firm was addressing was becoming undifferentiated. That is to say, the firm was offering the same range of products to their entire customer base (banks, insurance agencies, investment firms, corporations, etc.) without due consideration for their specific industry-related needs. In addition, as this dedifferentiation process was proceeding from the point of view of the firm, they were losing sight of their customer needs for other new products.

The solution: The firm had grown in love with their product line, which in fact was to be envied. The result, however, was that a focus on the customer was lost as well as an in-depth sense of what they needed. The strategic planning process indicated that, in fact, the firm really had three customer types: financial institutions, corporations, and government. The redesign then entailed that their "front end"—that is, their "spearhead" into the marketplace—be threefold, based on these customer niches.

Another example will further illustrate how knowing your customer can be crucial to the bottom line:

The problem: A firm supplied large medical equipment to hospitals, care centers, and so on. Their problem was that the cost of inventory (of both parts and equipment) was eroding their margins, quality issues and similar issues were emerging, along with a growing failure to deliver service on time. Their firm's structure was traditional, with each department being its own "silo."

Historically, marketing's discovery of new markets led to sales selling any new product they could get a hold of (which was most financially rewarding for the sales people). The net result was a lack of "family of products" and, therefore, an absence of standardized parts, a need for an ever-increasing number of service personnel, and an ever-growing need for increased training of service personnel. The firm had never really determined what their customers needed in the way of equipment, nor had they determined who their "best" customers were.

The solution: Creating four ad hoc cross-functional teams, each led by a representative of a major department and meeting regularly. The teams carried the designations common in industry—marketing, sales, service, and purchasing. Each team focused on who their customer was, is, and should be and what could be in the best interest of their unit. For example, the service team (composed of representatives from each discipline and headed by a service representative) had equal input as the marketing team as to which customer niche should be targeted. They offered the characteristics of an ideal customer based on repair rates, additional services required, machine capabilities, and so on. Marketing had the necessary constraints placed on where they could go to find customer niches. Purchasing could focus on the equipment that the firm's ideal customer needed and not waste time and money buying costly product that didn't yield much profit.

The value of having four teams meeting regularly allowed each department to have their requirements scrutinized and updated in a timely fashion before cost overruns and inefficiencies developed. The net result for the firm was a healthy profit picture to which each department contributed.

Interestingly enough, the few customers who left to buy elsewhere turned out to be the least profitable for the company.

A third example shows how changing the interface with the firm's customer base can overcome a firm's failure to grow.

The problem: The growth of a large accounting firm had stagnated, accompanied by a growing restlessness among junior members who were not attaining partnership status as rapidly as they had been promised. An organizational audit indicated that each of the firm's departments (audit, tax, consulting, etc.) operated as independent entities with little cross-selling or collaboration. In addition, the marketing message of the firm was indistinct and the intended audience was nondescript. Lastly, junior accountants were left to their own devices when it came to "rainmaking"—their lack of success in this area contributed to the low level of partnership invitations.

The solution: The firm was reorganized into industry groups with each function and service represented in each group. This did not mean that accountants had to surrender clients who were not in their industry group, nor did it mean they could not pursue clients in other industries. It did mean, though, that the members of a group had to focus their efforts on that industry: joining trade associations, writing articles for trade journals, presenting at association conventions, advertising to that industry, and so on. Cross-selling and joint-selling was emphasized and rewarded. Junior accountants assigned to a group were mentored by the partners in that group and were taught how to "make rain."

Subsequently, the firm became known as the experts in the focal industries chosen. Their growth resumed. Most important was that the firm widened its services to any one customer's range of needs so that revenues from any one customer increased accordingly. Junior accountants felt more directed in their efforts, and the rate of partnership growth increased.

The focus in each one of these examples is on the design changes at the interface of the firm and its customers. After all, it is the customer that drives the business. Organizations risk failure in not considering how they go to market—that is, in how they address and service their customers. They face an even greater threat when not designing their company to expedite and facilitate this process—that is, in not delivering the products and services their customers want, when they want them, and in what form they want them.

The "front end" of the company (the interface with customers) is emphasized here, in comparison to the "back end" where operations and administration occur, only to highlight how crucial customer definition, selection, and service is for design efforts. The overlap is considerable since the design of the interface effects how the "back end" is constructed. Redesign efforts require adjustment throughout the firm in order to efficiently and productively support the "front."

The overriding principle in design efforts is enhancing the flow of customer information throughout the firm—ensuring that the necessary channels of communication are in place and that they direct the necessary data to the proper departments. This is the primary goal of design efforts.

The Small Change That Convinces

As indicated earlier, a major first step of the middle phase is the selection of a "small change," not a grand redesign of the organization. What can solidify staff's commitment to the organization of the future are immediate "wins" that impress, wins that say, "We are on track." Which small initiatives to choose will depend on the model of the flexible organization you have developed and what immediate steps need to be taken along that path. It is important that the "small win" be a natural outgrowth of your overall strategy since the aim is to garner support and enthusiasm for your future plans. The choice should be one that your management team sees as both significant and doable. A "small win" may not guarantee you'll have a successful harvest, but it raises the probability.

Laying the groundwork for "the small change that convinces" and its success is dependent on at least four factors:

1. A strategic statement that provides the next steps to take in ensuring your firm is flexible enough to overcome whatever challenges the future holds.
2. Developing a Balanced Scorecard and a picture of how to enhance information flow throughout the organization.
3. The collaboration of your management team in deciding which initiative will be the showcase.
4. Celebrating the success of the showcase change.

We have previously discussed the first three items. The fourth, celebrating victories, makes it all worthwhile. Who does not want to be part of a winning team? Who does not want to know that their team is competent enough and able to pull it off? Who does not want to know that their team stands a very good chance of surviving the undecipherable future, if not thriving in it?

And who does not want to be recognized for contributing to a victory? Who does not want to be known as the one that saved the day when the team took a wrong turn that could have turned into a disaster? Who does not want to feel that their skills were needed for the victory to occur?

Celebrating both the group and individual in the firm's victory elevates the spirit and enhances the loyalty to and identification with the organization. Perhaps most important, it smoothes the way for other future changes that may be needed. It reduces resistance. In fact, it can introduce the staff's desire for more change and welcome it!

Self-Reflection: The Major Task of the Middle Phase

Utilize your management team in responding to the following questions:

1. What are the driving forces that affect your industry and your firm? If you are a division of an organization or a department within a

larger organization, there are two types of driving forces: the forces internal to your organization that affect your area of responsibility and those that impact the company as a whole.

2. Describe the scenarios that you and your team create for the issue under consideration (e.g., for strategic planning, to decide on a particular course of action, to parse the impact a product introduction might have). Include the following for each scenario:

    a. How the driving forces change their direction and combine to create the scenario

    b. A storyline, including a history of events dating from today to the occurrence of the scenario

    c. A description of how your firm is able to thrive in each scenario

    d. A description of your competitors (imagined or real) and how they are managing in each scenario. Ensure that the strategies you and your competitors have chosen are distinctly different from each other. This directive is intended to support "out-of-the-box" thinking

    e. What common themes have your uncovered? What new possibilities have been stimulated?

    f. What route to the future have you and your team determined is the one for you?

    g. What do you have to start doing now in order to begin the journey?

    h. What key markers along the road need to be in place so that you and your team know you either are on the right track or, alternatively, need to change directions?

3. What is the distinctive strategy you and your team have created that will guide your organization into the future?

4. Develop a Balanced Scorecard of objectives, measures, and goals and their interrelationships.

5. Diagram how customer information flows through your organization. Where does the "ball" get dropped? How can these errors be eliminated?

6. What is the "small change that convinces"? Why has this been chosen versus other potential candidates?

7. How well has it done to influence staff's commitment to the new strategy?

CHAPTER 6

Implementing and Settling In

Success can lead to failure!

That statement sounds either like one of those simple-minded slogans used to motivate people to stay alert, a truism that really isn't very instructive, or a meaningless string of words. But we all have seen examples of success (e.g., in organizations and careers, with products) followed by, if not leading to, failure and defeat.

Success does not necessarily, much less inevitably, cause failure, nor is success the direct cause of failure in any specific case. However, with success, organizations can become complacent about the future ("We are so good that nothing can harm us!"). Management can become so absorbed in ensuring that work gets done that they don't look up ("We are too busy dealing with the day-to-day demands to do a strategic plan!"). Success can wed businesses to one view so much so that they exclude everything else ("Why mess with success?"). Success can bring out the best in competitors, leaving previously successful organizations in the dust ("Their product can't touch us or our market share!").

Similar blind spots can occur for individual managers and executives who have flourished in making the transition from "newly appointed" to "executive in fact." Success can breed complacency, absorption in day-to-day activities, rigidness in outlook, a failure to see what is gaining on you, and so on.

The question then becomes, "How can I protect myself and my team against these blind spots?" This workbook has emphasized relying on your staff and others for input, perspective, and ideas while simultaneously and judiciously offering them insight into your style, your thinking process, and your points of view. In order for both parties—that is, you and your staff—to be up to the task of eliminating blind spots, the value of each partner has to be continually enhanced.

Augmenting Your Value

It is difficult to think of anything more valuable to your firm than your engagement in continuous learning. Consider what your new learning can bring on behalf of your company. Reflect on the model of behavior your staff can emulate. Consultants and executives have been exposed over many years to the concept of the "learning company."[1] If there is such a thing, it assuredly begins with you the leader.

Maurer and Weiss[2] have suggested that continuous learning is a process that entails the following:

- A learning orientation
- Your inner work standards
- An ability to recognize your strengths and weaknesses
- An ability to learn new things

Learning Orientation

Seeking developmental activities and wanting to expand one's skills, interests, and knowledge reflect your learning orientation. Learning new things about your organization, its marketplace, and the industry are examples. Given that your professional background is in marketing, you investigate finance. Going beyond the immediacy of your business, a learning orientation might drive you to explore in more depth decision-making principles or system dynamics—topics that have been touched upon in this workbook. New learning can virtually be about anything—a new type of machinery, the financials of "price transfer" involving your department, innovative methods of assessing talent, and so on. It can include a new viewpoint that you import from a class that you have taken. No matter what, new learning can only strengthen the contribution of your decision making to the success of your department. In general, a learning orientation takes you to places you know little about initially but that pique your interest.

Personal Work Standards

As Maurer and Weiss[3] suggest, "Individuals with high inner work standards will strive to do their best, even when a lesser level of performance would be acceptable." They further provide an analysis of the psychological dynamics of an individual with high work standards by contrasting two images the individual has of himself or herself—the possible ideal self and the actual self. The individual portrayed is continually striving toward the ideal self and in doing so is propelled out of his or her usual mode of operating. Dynamics such as these are usually accompanied by a self-critical attitude. However, self-criticism can become self-flagellation and can easily draw others into its web, making this behavior both destructive and demoralizing for self and others. What guards against this extreme is the next component of continuous learning, self-objectivity.

Self-Objectivity

Recognizing one's strengths and weaknesses has been a leitmotif either directly or implicitly discussed throughout this workbook. In the context of continuous learning, its importance resides in knowing one's developmental deficiencies and those that require improvement. It can serve as a map for one direction new learning might take.

Other than the individuals who are entirely satisfied with the status quo and have no desire whatsoever to change themselves or their situations, most of us harbor a desire to grow and develop. The impetus for this arises from some combination of internal motivation (e.g., ambition, boredom, feeling challenged) and external happenstance (e.g., a job opening that is appealing, a crisis that demands a unique and different approach, a failure that requires repair). Internal motivation and external circumstance go hand in glove, though it is difficult to assess in what measure. Thus, an executive might want to learn how to deal with conflict in the absence of an immediate, ostensible need while feeling that developing this skill may enhance his chances for advancement or poorly handling a disagreeable conflict situation might impress on the executive the need to develop this skill. Both cases reflect this duality—the internal ambition for advancement in an external situation where advancement is a possibility and the internal wish or need to succeed in the external crisis situation.

The focus on this duality provides assistance to an individual in deciding which development issues to address and in what priority. The choice depends on both circumstance (what is either immediately necessary or what you know the future will bring) and motivation. Keeping in mind this duality will support both what has to be learned and how learning will widen your perspective.

Ability to Learn

Our earlier discussion (chapter 2) on decision making posed four questions: where do we look for the facts that we use in decision making, what determines where we look for these facts, what influences how we look, and how do we understand what we see and find. Our ability to learn is heavily dependent on how we answer these four questions and how our behavior mirrors our answers. To the extent that we can question and examine the "how" (linear vs. system thinking), the "where" (our mental models and basic assumptions), the "what" (our biases), and our understanding processes (sense making), to that extent we learn. Short of that we are simply repeating what we have previously experienced and thought even in the face of new challenges.

In addition to attending to these four elements of a continuous learning style, the extent to which you interact with other social and organizational entities can broaden the impact of your new learning on your organization. This involves both telling and listening—telling others about your needs, concerns, wishes, plans, strategy, and so on and asking for and listening to theirs. The benefits are abundant. Not only do you get to hear about the events in other divisions and organizations that could affect yours, but you also have the opportunity to engage prospective partners in some of your initiatives. Further, to the degree that your networking is successful, you are able to enlist others' identification with you, your organization, and your plans.

Boosting the Value of Your Staff

In General

The more involved, committed, and informed your staff is, the more you will be privy to the requisite variety of opinions and outlooks that will keep your vision clear. To create this kind of staff requires that they have both the desire and the opportunities to expand and test out their understanding of what it takes for the company to succeed and how they can contribute to that victory. It is up to you to serve these nourishing helpings as well as encourage people to partake.

What you can do is divided into several broad activities among many others:

- Celebrate achievement, progress, and success on the individual, team, department, division, and company-wide level:
  - Rewarding achievement and progress
  - Team building
  - Promoting innovation, creativity, and "out-of-the-box" thinking
  - Communicating events, decisions, changes, and so on
  - Soliciting feedback about the organization
- Provide training opportunities:
  - Technical (related to the specific job)
  - Professional (e.g., enhancing decision-making skills, leadership development, supervisory programs)
  - Personal (e.g., individualized coaching opportunities)

Each of these undertakings is equally crucial not only in the early stages of your transition but also during your entire tenure as executive. These efforts can be solidified by a development program that is consciously designed for each employee. The message this sends is that each person is valuable to the organization, that their value increases the more training they receive, and therefore, that a development program for each employee is a necessity for the continued growth of the organization.

Your managers and supervisors might develop a record for each employee along the following lines:

- Strengths
- Weaknesses
- Developmental needs
- Training classes taken
- Training classes suggested

Further, this kind of information prepares each department within your organization to deal with future events, events such as not enough talent to undertake the firm's mission, talent that is so stretched that a person leaving can upset progress, talent that needs to be developed to handle new products, a different strategic approach, and so on.

Coaching Your Managers to Become Coaches

Developing a culture of employee commitment and organizational identification obviously takes a great deal of work and effort, and it starts at the top. How you as CEO or senior executive enact your role is a major contributor to the kind of culture that ensues. Your management team is part of the "top" as well, and their behavior toward employees shares the credit for the culture that develops. So much of management's relationship with their staff reflects your relationship with management.

An earlier section (chapter 4) highlighted some aspects of this relationship, particularly those elements that an executive arriving in a new position might witness and need to deal with. Also, our discussion about your teachable point of view as an expression of how you see a business thriving added another dimension to your relationship with your management team.

Another influence is one that is rarely mentioned yet has the potential to be the most significant: coaching your managers to become coaches to their staff. In undertaking this responsibility, you are not only assisting your managers in their personal development but also serving as a role model for how your managers should relate to their respective teams. One of the many factors that has been recognized as a hallmark of successful management behavior is the ability to develop the members of their team.

However, the design in the majority of management-development programs omits the details of how executives and managers are to accomplish staff development though their performance evaluation frequently includes how well they perform in this respect. In general, these programs expand upon the knowledge base of executives. In addition to technical and industry-specific knowledge, emphasis is usually placed on individual and team psychological theory. Frequently, feedback to the individual executive (in the form of 360 degrees and management-assessment instruments) is part of these programs. The intent of most management-development programs is to broaden the individual's view of what constitutes good management practices, with the expectation that the insight the executive acquires will lead to the development of talent among his or her staff. He or she is expected to apply this knowledge without further training. To repeat, what is not stressed is the formal coaching of these future leaders in the "how" of developing the talent of staff members.

Frequently internal and external consultants are called upon to train staff on behalf of the management team, inadvertently depriving executives and managers the opportunity to expand their skills in this area. The implication of this practice is not so much that these tasks are beyond the ability of executives and managers (though in some cases they may be), but that it is assumed that they are too busy to learn these skills. They have other things to do that are more directly pertinent to their responsibilities. In other words, one of the most powerful tools management has—to develop staff—is delegated to others.

What do you need to know to become a coach to the members of your management team? In order to answer this question, let's first explore some of the features of a coaching relationship that a trained coach considers crucial. Coaching is a process based on a developing relationship where the following occurs:

- The more the person being coached (the manager) feels that he or she can trust the coach (to be helpful, to have his or her best interests at the forefront, etc.), the more he or she can utilize the coach as a sounding board (for thoughts not expressed, feelings not acknowledged, etc.) and take advantage of the feedback the coach (you, the executive) offers.
- The more accepting (as opposed to being judgmental) the coach is of the manager, the more he or she can value the strengths of the manager.

- The more these two simultaneously occurring states grow, the broader the behavioral and psychological arena that the manager can explore in him or herself becomes.
- The broader this arena grows, the more strengths and skills are discovered and the more creative the manager becomes (in decision making, problem solving, learning, etc.).

There are at least two responsibilities of the executive that interfere with the coaching process:

1. The executive has to evaluate staff members and judge their performance and competency.
2. The executive is responsible for achieving the strategic goals assigned to his or her department.

These responsibilities can result in a host of contradictory aims.

- How can an executive or coach elicit the kind of trust that is a coach's mainstay when the staff members know that the coach is also evaluating them?
- How difficult is it for executives to invest time and energy in a manager they find to be an underperformer when the pressure is on them to get the work out?
- Will staff members, knowing that their executive is being evaluated (by the firm's board) on the basis of his or her ability to develop staff, use this to control the executive?

There are many other questions that arise because there is an apparently inherent conflict of interest in the dual role of executive and coach. How can an executive overcome these obstacles?

The one commonality shared by a coach and an executive acting as a coach that both utilize to attain their goals is making meaningful assignments and debriefing the results. This is one aspect of coaching that both an executive acting as a coach and a professional coach utilize: the former in a much more formal, structured, and influential fashion than the latter. Their respective sets of assignments are understandably of a different magnitude with respect to the welfare of the company.

For example, the professional coach assigns "homework" tasks that have to do with interpersonal relations, self-organization, handling assignments—all very important in the personal development of the manager. On the other hand, the assignments made by the executive coach have to do with creating a new department, turning around the fortunes of a division, implementing a strategic design, restructuring a department, and so on.[4] What they both share is the enormous value that comes from debriefing the staff members' actions after the fact. For professional coaches the debriefing is the most fundamental, if not the most definitive, means of evaluating progress and planning interventions. This also holds true for the executive coach in his or her work with staff. The insights the managers derive from feedback in debriefing sessions with either the professional coach or the executive coach is a crucial element in the managers' development.

The in-depth discussion between the executive coach and managers regarding how the latter went about solving a problem, undertaking a project, or creating a team can yield important insights regarding the managers' personal styles as leaders, their thinking processes when assessing a difficult situation, their general method of problem solving, their usual assumptions when evaluating different types of situations, and so on. Bringing these issues to the forefront allows the manager to make the necessary adjustments that allow for continued professional development. What is required, however, is a skilled executive coach whose focus is precisely on these types of issues.

In contrast is the typical debriefing by an executive of a manager's behavior in an assignment. The spotlight is usually exclusively on the end product, the result. Rarely will an executive parse the specific actions taken by his or her manager. The executive's stance is understandable— he or she is responsible for the performance of his or her division, and the assignment's main function is to contribute to that. On the other hand, the executive coach has to consider both functions—the end result and staff development. It is the executive coach's ability to delve into the managers' mental models and extract their underlying assumptions; that is the hallmark of an executive coach.

Though it takes experience and practice to be artful in debriefing managers, try employing a variation of the frames described in the earlier section on decision making in chapter 2.

- Describe how and why you did what you did in this situation.
- What was your picture of the ideal outcome that governed how you went about dealing with the situation?
- How else could you have managed the situation successfully? Describe in detail what would have led to what. (Even if the manager doesn't immediately see another way, insist that he or she create a possible way. Not being able to see another way is itself diagnostic since usually there are other solutions to a problem.)
- Had you chosen this other way of handling the situation instead of the method you actually did, imagine why you would have done so.

Self-Reflection

Augmenting Your Value

1. What have you learned about your company that you hadn't known before? Consider sorting your new learning into different categories, the intent being to make sure that you don't focus on one topic (e.g., finance) to the exclusion of the others. Falling into this trap will surely tighten the blinders. A category system might include the following: processes, people and teams, your marketplace, strategy, and finance.

2. What have you learned about other divisions or companies that you hadn't known before?

3. With which department(s) and organizations have you been in contact? What was the nature of the interaction? What implications are there for your department from the interaction(s)?

4. With which departments and organizations have you intended to be in contact but have not been? Why not? (Don't use the excuse of not having enough time. If other interactions deserve priority listing, then explain why these do not.)

5. Make a case for networking with those departments and organizations with whom you feel you need not. You might surprise yourself.

6. With which senior staff (superiors) have you been in contact? What was discussed? What did they tell you about their plans, the company,

your department's role in the future of the firm, and so on? What implications does this have for you?

7. Collating what you have learned in answering these questions, how can you apply this to the benefit of your company, division, or department? What might you and your department do differently to benefit from the insight you have derived from interacting with these various entities?

Boosting the Value of Your Staff

8. Deliberately keep a record of significant successes that you and your staff celebrate and whom the success is for (person, department, level within the organization). The reason for this is to ensure not only that celebration is occurring but also that it is for everyone in the firm. Too often certain groups and individuals are overlooked.

9. Develop a "talent scorecard" that you discuss with your management team and disseminate throughout your organization. The intent is to both develop the individual and ensure the preparedness of the organization for the future.

CHAPTER 7

Throughout the Process

We all tend to be absorbed in the work in front of us, to concentrate on the problems and challenges of the moment, and to concentrate on what we can do about them. In this pressurized context we will predictably revert to our usual, preferred, and stylistic ways of operating and responding. What exacerbates this pull is any newly appointed executive wanting to do well and demonstrate that being chosen was indeed the right move on the part of the powers that be. Since our past successful assignments are usually the basis of our appointment to this new position, we rely on what got us here—that is, our usual way of doing things. When we do find the time to raise our heads out of the mire of these immediate demands, some of us just go on to the next task that we anticipate will emerge, some take the proverbial sigh of relief and go out to dinner, others will obsess about what they could have done better—the reactions are numerous.

To the extent that we wait for the current confluence of issues (the mire referenced previously) to end before we pull our heads out and up, to that extent we diminish our effectiveness in the new position. One way of looking at this workbook is to view it as a series of tasks, vantage points, perspectives, thought-questions, and suggestions that pull you away from your usual way of conducting business and offer you alternative perspectives that can be applied to your current situation. The message being conveyed is that being overly absorbed in the moment can detract from the best decisions you can make, the best choice of behavior that can get you what you want and where you want to go. Remaining aware of alternatives to your usual mode of behaving, different perspectives, and ways of perceiving may not offer you salvation but will surely improve your chances of success in your new position. This is the attitude we preach that should be adopted throughout your career. The first few phases of your new assignment are the occasions to practice this attitude.

When we are absorbed in the moment, we typically bring our previous way of operating, our style, to the occasion. The continuum along which we have observed new executives respond to their new assignment ranges from doing as little as possible, a passive response to their new situation, to doing too much all at once. In looking back on how these executives have responded to new situations in the past, these responses stand out.

From a cognitive point of view, passivity can result from the lack of an internalized criterion for determining when action is required. From a psychological point of view, passivity follows a fear of doing wrong and being found out. The combination of the cognitive and the psychological act to produce the position that it is better to not commit oneself and not act than to decide to do something, something that might be demonstrably wrong. After all, a problem that developed from not doing something can be excused by "I didn't know." At the other end of the continuum is the desire to immediately fix everything you see as wrong. A basic motive for this desire to fix is the fear that you will be seen as lacking if everything isn't already shipshape or on the road to that state. However, feeling the need to react at once invites us to react with our usual style that is mindless of other approaches and viewpoints.

This last chapter then is an invitation to review the material useful in freeing you from total absorption in day-to-day demands. The chapter invites you, once again, to adopt a self-critical stance toward the decisions you make, the programs you oversee, and the planning you do.

We have stressed throughout this workbook that there will always be a discrepancy, major or minor, between how we see ourselves and how others see us, between what we think we are conveying and how it appears to others. One significant method of keeping track of these discrepancies and attempting to reduce them is to keep a running record of our written responses (http://www.businessexpertpress.com/liebowitz) to the questions raised at the end of the chapters and periodically reviewing them. Our responses will change over time and will reveal what we have learned (about ourselves and our business) during that period. The value of this retrospective review lies in the evolution of your ideas and what you can learn from it. It will reveal earlier assumptions that have changed, perceptions that have matured, and insights that have been gained, all of which can contribute to an increased insight into ourselves that will stand us in good stead in the future.

One dramatic impact self-insight can effect is an awareness of the constraints we impose on ourselves in our decision making. Fact-finding is the basis of decision making, but it is not simply a matter of observing facts and then utilizing them to bolster an argument. Our biases and assumptions appear at first glance as almost instinctive and for that very reason have to be brought into the light and revised to accommodate the situation.

Your Tasks

The case has been made for certain tasks to be undertaken in overlapping phases of the early months. These include the period in which you and the board are deciding whether you are the one for the position, the initial phase, a middle period, and then the final one that extends into the future.

Accepting an offer to head a company or division implies your awareness of the accompanying expectations, whether implicitly or explicitly stated, that you introduce change and that the change will enhance the firm's functioning. All the more then that, in accepting the offer, you need to be very clear and specific about the board's criteria of performance and the boundaries (e.g., who can you replace if necessary, what strategic directions you can adopt) within which you can operate.

As important as being clear about the expectations the board has of you is your awareness of how you fit within the organization. Determination of fit includes not only your compatibility with the organization's culture, but also how well your abilities and skills match the firm's immediate and future needs. Thus, for example, a firm needing to be turned around may be the downfall of a CEO who finds it difficult to make rapid decisions about whether to retain personnel.

The initial period is a time to be devoted to analysis of the business itself, the management team, the key players, and the networking within and outside of the organization. This stage also entails the firm getting to know you and your philosophy of business—that is, your teachable point of view. Not only is this a time for getting acquainted, but it also sets the stage for determining how you and your team will work together, establishing your credibility, and defining how successful the change efforts will be.

The challenges of the middle phase include the actual beginnings of the change process. This not only involves determining the "small change" that by its success can energize the workforce but also involves the overall strategy within which the small change is nested. Setting a strategy requires considering how it will be implemented (performance management), as well as the organization design that will enhance its chances for success.

The fourth stage extends well into the future. Its tasks and responsibilities have to do with expanding and enhancing both your value and your team's value to the organization. The challenge of this period is to expand your learning and personal development while attending to the professional development of your team members. One of your most important tasks during this period is becoming a coach to your management team, enabling them, in turn, to become coaches to their staff.

It is not ironic that the final statement is about you—your development and learning. After all, the success of your tenure in this new assignment is up to you.

Self-Reflection

1. What have you learned about yourself?
2. What are you learning about yourself?
3. What do you have yet to learn about?

Notes

Chapter 1

1. Ciampa and Watkins (1999); Watkins (2003).
2. Watkins (2003).
3. Barnett and Tichy (2000).
4. Barnett and Tichy (2000), pp. 17–18.
5. Barnett and Tichy (2000), p. 19.
6. Nadler (2007), pp. 69ff.

Chapter 2

1. Savage and Oliphant (2009).
2. Sterman (2000), p. 13.
3. Lakoff and Johnson (1980).
4. Lakoff and Johnson (1980), p. 33.
5. Lakoff and Johnson (1980), p. 4.
6. Morgan (2006).
7. Morgan (2006), p. 72.
8. Morgan (2006), pp. 115ff.
9. Bazerman and Moore (2009), pp. 3–4.
10. Bazerman and Moore (2009), p. 3.
11. Bazerman and Moore (2009), p. 40.
12. Bazerman and Moore (2009), p. 41.
13. Weick (1995).
14. Weick (1995), p. 11.
15. Weick (1995), p. 10.
16. Weick (1995), p. 17.
17. Weick (1995), p. 78.
18. Weick (1995), p. 31.
19. Harvey (1974).
20. Harvey (1974), p. 43.

Chapter 3

1. Simons (2005), pp. 17–30.
2. Borgatti (2001).
3. Lange (1991).
4. Deal and Kennedy (1982), pp. 107–127.
5. Morgan (2006).
6. Ashkanasy, Broadfoot, and Falkus (2000).
7. Dalton et al. (1997).

Chapter 5

1. Kaplan and Norton (1996); Kaplan and Norton (2004).
2. Schwartz (1991).
3. Ringland (1998); Fahey and Randall (1998).
4. Kaplan and Norton (1996); Kaplan and Norton (2004).
5. Kaplan and Norton (2004), p. 10.
6. Mintzberg (1983), chap. 11.
7. Galbraith (1995).

Chapter 6

1. Senge (1990), p. 503.
2. Maurer and Weiss (2009), p. 2.
3. Maurer and Weiss (2009), p. 8.
4. Dalton et al. (1997), pp. v–16.

References

Ashkanasy, N. M., Broadfoot, L. E., & Falkus, S. (2000). Organizational measures of organizational culture. In N. M. Ashkanasy, C. P. M. Wilderom, & M. F. Peterson (Eds.), *Handbook of organizational culture & climate* (pp. 131–145). Thousand Oaks, CA: Sage.

Barnett, C. K., & Tichy, N. (2000). Rapid-cycle CEO development: How new leaders learn to take charge. *Organizational Dynamics, 28*(1), 16–32.

Bazerman, M. H., & Moore, D. A. (2009). *Judgment in managerial decision making.* Hoboken, NJ: John Wiley & Sons.

Borgatti, S. (2001). Introduction to organizational behavior. Retrieved from http://www.analytictech.com/mb021/index.htm

Ciampa, D., & Watkins, M. (1999). *Right from the start: Taking charge in a new leadership role.* Boston, MA: Harvard Business School Press.

Dalton, M., Lombardo, M., McCauley, C., McDonald-Mann, D., Moxley, R., & Wachholz, L. (1997). *Benchmarks: Developmental reference points. A manual and trainer's guide.* Greensboro, NC: Center for Creative Leadership

Deal, T. E., & Kennedy, A. A. (1982). *Corporate cultures: The rites and rituals of corporate life.* Reading, MA: Addison Wesley Publishing Company.

Fahey, L., & Randall, R. M. (Eds.). (1998). *Learning from the future: Competitive foresight scenarios.* New York, NY: John Wiley & Sons.

Galbraith, J. R. (1995). *Designing organizations: An executive briefing on strategy, structure and process.* San Francisco, CA: Jossey-Bass.

Harvey, J. (1974). The Abilene paradox: The management of agreement. *Organizational Dynamics,* 63–80.

Kaplan, R. S., & Norton, D. (1996). *The balanced scorecard: Translating strategy into action.* Boston, MA: Harvard Business School Press.

Kaplan, R. S., & Norton, D. (2004). *Strategy maps: Converting intangible assets into tangible outcomes.* Boston, MA: Harvard Business School Press.

Lakoff, G., & Johnson, M. (1980). *Metaphors we live by.* Chicago, IL: University of Chicago Press.

Lange, C. (1991, July 1). Ritual in business: Building a corporate culture through symbolic management. *Industrial Management.* Retrieved from http://www.thefreelibrary.com/Ritual+in+business%3a+building+a+corporate+culture+through+symbolic+management.-a01128986

Maurer, T. J., & Weiss, E. M. (2009, July). Continuous learning skill demands: Associations with managerial job content, age, and experience. *Journal of Business Psychology*. doi:10.1007/sl0869-009-9126-0

Mintzberg, H. (1983). *Designing effective organizations: Structure in fives*. Englewood Cliffs, NJ: Prentice Hall.

Morgan, G. (2006). *Images of organization*. Thousand Oaks, CA: Sage.

Nadler, D. A. (2007). The CEOs second act. *Harvard Business Review, 85*(1), 66–72.

Ringland, G. (1998). *Scenario planning: Managing for the future*. New York, NY: John Wiley & Sons.

Savage, D. G., & Oliphant, J. (2009, July 15). Sotomayor answers her Senate critics in hearing. *Los Angeles Times*.

Schwartz, P. (1991). *The art of the long view*. New York, NY: Doubleday Currency.

Senge, P. M. (1990). *The fifth discipline: The art & practice of the learning organization*. New York, NY: Currency Doubleday.

Simons, R. (2005). *Levers of organization design: How managers use accountability systems for greater performance and commitment*. Boston, MA: Harvard Business School Press.

Sterman, J. D. (2000). *Business dynamic: Systems thinking and modeling for a complex world*. Boston, MA: Irwin McGraw-Hill.

Weick, K. E. (1995). *Sensemaking in organizations*. Thousand Oaks, CA: Sage.

Index